Trinidad Express

Sailing from South Africa to Trinidad

Second Edition

By

James E. Keen

Two sailors on a 36-foot sailboat make a speedy 5,400 nautical mile ocean voyage from South Africa to Saint Helena Island, to Fernando de Noronha, Brazil, and finally to Trinidad.

Library of Congress Control Number: 2012940522

Library of Congress Cataloging-in-Publication Data
Keen, James., 1942- Trinidad Express: Sailing from South
Africa to Trinidad / James E. Keen, Includes biographical
References and indcx.
p. cm.

ISBN-13: 978-1539969266

1. Sailing – blue water, 2. Southern Atlantic Ocean, 3. Cruising and Voyaging, 4. South Africa, 5. Saint Helena Island, 6. Fernando de Noronha. 7. Trinidad, James E. I. Title.

Published in the United States by:

Beaufort Press
252-946-8305
Cover design by Dana Newbrough

Second Edition Printed in the United States of America by
CreateSpace, of On-Demand Publishing LLC, part of the
Amazon group of companies

Dedication

In Memory of Bert Herring, my friend.

Bert was a colleague and keeper of our college computer system. He was a biblical scholar, an armchair sailor, a lover of knowledge he gained from extensive reading, and a devout man with an understanding, loving wife, children, and many grandchildren.

He was eager to sail and shared a week aboard during my America's Great Loop adventure, providing knowledge and excitement.

He retired to live near the ocean and left us too soon.

Acknowledgements

Bill Doar and I play major roles in this adventure. I have tried to remember other major players; however, please accept my apologies and thanks if I fail to mention you.

My thanks to the following people for participation in this chronicle:

- Bill Doar: for allowing me to use his personal email dispatches and for correcting, encouraging, editing, and being a good sport about this book.
- Jackie Keen, my wife: for her editing, patience, encouragement, and new ideas.
- Normandie Doar: as the true First Mate on Advent II.
- Dr. Buck Rish, author: for fabulous editing and mentoring a novice writer.
- Lane (poet and author) and Fred Schroeder: for edits, suggestions, and comments.
- Herta Abarr, author: for edits and comments.
- Tia Bach, author, blogger, and my formal book editor: for smoothing the rough edges.
- Dana Newbrough, graphic designer: for a great book cover.
- Angela Silverthorne, author: for being a friend, advisor, and purveyor of good advice.
- Pamlico Writers Group: for advice and support.

Table of Contents

Prologue

Circumnavigation of the earth by Bill and Normandie Doar aboard their thirty-six-foot custom steel French sailing sloop Advent II started in 2003. They sailed south from North Carolina, into the Atlantic Ocean to the Caribbean, then westward through the Panama Canal, across the Pacific Ocean, across Australia via the Coral Sea, the Arafura Sea, the Timor Sea, and finally across the Indian Ocean to the shores of South Africa in December 2004.

As their cruising kitty dwindled, their shared plans changed. Normandie would resume her work as a nurse in North Carolina and attend school to become a nurse anesthetist. This plan would provide funds for Bill to complete the trip.

Although Bill was competent to sail alone, the precarious and lonely 5,400-mile ocean crossing aboard Advent II to reach Trinidad, cross her outgoing track, and complete the circumnavigation would not be wise without a first mate.

Bill's daughter Grayson planned to get married during Easter 2005 in Charleston, SC. Bill had promised to give the bride away, a commitment that dictated a tight schedule for the Atlantic crossing.

At Trinidad, Bill would haul the boat into storage and fly home for the wedding. He would return and leisurely sail singlehandedly north from the Caribbean islands to North Carolina.

James E. Keen

* * * * * *

I was approaching retirement after a career as a community college professor. My youth had been spent reading books about ocean voyaging and dreaming of making an ocean crossing. I sailed most of my life in North Carolina coastal waters, currently enjoying my boat Irish Mist, a thirty-two-foot sailing sloop. Although I had sailed offshore many times, I had spent only a few nights on ocean passages.

A colleague, who was following Bill and Normandie's trek via the internet, suggested I contact Bill about joining Advent II as crew. After some research, I realized the couple was my neighbor in Chocowinity, NC. A friend knew them to be quality people, emergency medical technicians, and members of Trinity Episcopal Church. Bill and I were about the same age.

My wife, Jackie, agreed to allow me to volunteer for the crossing. I sent Bill a tentative introductory email including a brief outline of my sailing abilities. After several email exchanges, Bill wrote, "Jim, make sure you get a physical checkup and meet me in Cape Town, South Africa."

So it would happen—the completion of the circumnavigation. I became the First Mate on Advent II for an express crossing from South Africa to Trinidad, with short stops in Saint Helena Island and Fernando de Noronha, Brazil.

Welcome aboard for a ride on the Trinidad Express!

Chapter 1

South Africa: A Modern Country of Changes

 Sunday, Jan 9, 2005

Arriving in SA and Meeting Bill Doar

Career and family commitments had previously made me indefinitely postpone my dream of an ocean crossing. Now, retirement makes it possible.

The January 2005 flight from North Carolina to New York is smooth. The New York to London winter flight over the North Atlantic Ocean is bumpy for the tail rider in seat number 60D. The plane shakes violently but holds together.

After a short layover in London's Heathrow airport, I board a Virgin Atlantic Airlines flight to Cape Town, South Africa, with a cabin crew attending my every need.

My mood and thoughts are mixed.

I am greeted by a gorgeous orange-red South African sunrise with whitecaps on the dark ocean, 37,000 feet below. I know that if I can see the rough water from seven miles up, it is really rough on the surface. What have I gotten myself into?

In a few hours, I will meet Bill Doar and join his world of offshore cruising. He is used to a sailing life of offshore passage making, while I've only sailed protected North Carolina sounds and rivers, with occasional offshore hops.

Will I be a loose cannon? How will I react? Will I embarrass myself? Will I put the boat in danger?

* * * * * *

Cape Town International Airport has an undersized terminal for such a major city. Modern buildings shimmer under a clear, almost Carolina Blue sky. I walk across the tarmac from the plane and realize that my northern hemisphere winter has suddenly become late summer with the temperature in the seventies with a stiff breeze.

I find my bags, approach customs, and answer a couple of questions as I present my required eight-hundred-dollar return trip airline ticket.

"Welcome to South Africa."

My computer bag is securely hung from my shoulder as I grab two unopened soft-side duffels, walk down the concourse to find the Skipper among the crowd of welcoming faces.

* * * * * *

Captain Doar is six-foot-two-inches tall, slim, fit, tan, and wearing a recycled white dress shirt, khaki shorts, white socks, and worn out tennis shoes. His thin white hair is crew cut on top of a thin angular face with a neatly trimmed white beard. He carries an Aussie sailing hat is in his hand.

Later, I discover that Bill always wears a recycled white dress shirt when going into town. Maybe it is some sort of a private protest or just reflective of his frugal nature. His clothes are clean, well-worn, and serviceable.

"Hello Skipper," I say as we peruse each other for the first time.

We look like Mutt and Jeff. I'm a little over six feet tall with a full white beard and white hair that is thinning and longer, in a conservative style. My rotund three-hundred-pound frame is stuffed into jeans and a heavy long-sleeved shirt. I carry a jacket that is only appropriate for the winter weather I have left behind. The warmth and angst of the meeting begin to make me sweat.

My weight and pallor convey the sedentary life of an academic while Bill's active life as a construction engineer and world cruiser is obvious.

We are indeed different creatures. What will we talk about? Will there be any common ground between his construction background and my academic world of accounting?

Maybe our love of sailing will carry the day.

* * * * * *

Outside the terminal, we find James Doonan, our Rikkis (taxi) driver who is, without a doubt, driving one of the smallest minivans I have ever seen. James and Bill occupy the front seat while I overfill the back two seats with my bulk and bags.

The short ride on a modern superhighway through suburban Cape Town and other small towns takes us twenty-one miles to Simon's Town. Shack townships and lush neighborhoods are squashed side-by-side amid splashes of colorful flowers and greenery on the sides of the road that put our award-winning North Carolina Road Beautification Program to shame.

James talks with pride while pointing out sights of his country. When passing a hospital, he tells us that Dr. Christian Bernard performed the world's first heart transplant there. Near the South

African President's residence, he points out a building that housed Nelson Mandela during part of his lengthy imprisonment.

He talks about national politics, local issues, race relations, and the ethnicities of the South African people. The population is just over fifty million people with the majority being Black Africans (79.5%) speaking the native languages and controlling the government. The remainder includes: White (9%), composed of Afrikaans (Dutch) and English ancestry; Coloured (9%), a mixed race population who has

Meeting James Doonan at Cape Town Airport

some black ancestry but speak European-based languages and adopt western culture; and Indian/Asian (2.5%), descendants of imported Indian and Asian workers.

The South African currency is the Rand with a 2005 equivalence of R6.01 per U.S. dollar, making purchases appear expensive. I soon learn that costs are relative to currencies we encounter, with the values received nearly equal, except for fuel. Americans pay far less for fuel than most anywhere else in the world. Diesel fuel in South Africa is about four dollars per gallon.

South Africans speak a special flavor of English for commerce and governmental purposes, although the country has eleven official languages: Afrikaans, English, Ndebele, Northern Sotho, Sotho, Swazi, Tswana, Tsonga, Venda, Xhosa, and Zulu. Everyday English includes a heavy sprinkling of Afrikaans and African words. For example, robot is the word for traffic signals.

We circle the base of Table Mountain and cross a rather high mountain saddle, coasting downhill to see Valsbaai (False Bay) shimmering in the distance. Bill adds to James's constant informative chatter with, "It looks just like it does coming from the Golan Heights in the Syrian mountains, down to the Sea of Galilee."

False Bay is a large shallow body of water defined by Cape Hangklip on the east and Cape Point on the west. Earlier westbound mariners mistook Cape Hangklip for Cape Point and the numerous shipwrecks scattered about the bay bear their witness. False Bay earned its name as sailors misidentified the capes and erroneously entered the bay instead of the Atlantic Ocean.

James follows the British style, left-side driving four-lane boulevard through the village of Vishoek (Fish Hook), then along the bay shoreline. The ocean sparkles under the bright sun while a stiff wind blows spray from the tops of breaking waves onto the rocky shore.

As the shoreline bends to the east, we reach our destination.

* * * * * *

Simon's Town is a historic navy town where sailors mix with vacationing tourists from all over the world. The South African Navy Yard dominates the eastern end of town and its bulk provides shelter for the yacht club and town docks. Picturesque and heavily traveled Saint Georges Street parallels the bay and is lined with historic buildings.

Houses on the slopes of scraggy rock have magnificent northern views of the bay towards Vishoek while mysterious military buildings and antennas crown the adjacent arid mountaintop.

After descending a short, steep cobblestone driveway, we find our destination False Bay Yacht Club (FBYC) in a gated compound. Bill unlocks the security gate with an electronic key disc to find the yacht club building, a boatyard, and a ship's store sharing a site fronting the bay. Large boulders crowd the shoreline near the floating docks.

Bill's boat, Advent II, is berthed in the second-from-the-last slip on the last dock, very close to the big stone mole separating the club from the naval yard. The wind blasts me as I walk along the dock yet the clang of lines and halyards against sailboat masts is comforting and familiar. I follow Bill on the bouncing, snaking, floating dock while struggling to avoid falling. Anchoring gear from the bow-in moored boats surge in and out over the floating dock, moving with sea action to become obstacles to passage.

Advent II, a well found boat.

This is a wild place!

With the wind singing in the rigging, I collapse fully dressed across my bunk aboard Advent II. With little sleep in the past forty-eight hours, I sink into a much needed deep slumber.

Introducing Bill's Email Dispatches

Throughout their circumnavigation, Bill and Normandie used a distribution list to send email updates to friends and acquaintances. At infrequent intervals, when a fast internet connection was available, their website was updated with narratives and photos of the voyage.

Advent II is equipped with a high frequency, single sideband radio (SSB) that is controlled by the ship's laptop computer. Bill holds an amateur radio operator's license which allows him to use voice and data over the restricted radio bands. He maintains contact with cruisers' radio nets, weather forecasters, and other cruising boats.

I develop my own email distribution list of my work colleagues, relatives, and friends to keep them informed of our adventure. I type messages on my laptop and transfer them to the ship's computer for sending via the SSB. Daily thoughts and impressions are kept in my computer journal.

This is the first email dispatch Bill sends after I arrive.

Bill's Email Dispatch

Sunday, Jan 9, 2005, Simon's Town, South Africa

Jim Keen arrived this morning and spent the rest of the day getting acquainted with the boat and Simon's Town. He has been introduced to South African weather. Between 0600 hours when I left for the airport and 0900 hours when we got back, an unforecast windstorm moved in. It has been blowing in excess of 30 knots all day, but gustier than usual; hard blasts and relatively calm periods that last seconds at a time.

Tomorrow we will start the final preparations and get underway in a few days, weather permitting. This is the tentative schedule:

Leg #1, ETD 13 Jan. — Cape Town to Saint Helena (15°-50'S, 5°-50'W), 1,700 nautical miles, 17 days, ETA 30 January. Stay 5 days.

Leg #2, ETD 4 Feb — Saint Helena to Fernando de Noronha (3°-50'S, 32°-28'W), 1,800 nautical miles, 18 days, ETA 22 February. Stay 5 days.

Leg #3, ETD 27 Feb — Fernando de Noronha to Trinidad (10°-43'N, 61°-40'W), 2,000 nautical miles, 20 days, ETA 19 March.

It is a long way, but the wind and current are with us. The only tricky part is the first day or two out. We will need to get as far offshore as we can in case there is an unforecast gale, like today.

Getting to Know Modern SA

Bill wanted to show me around the country before getting down to the work of preparing for an offshore sea voyage of up to sixty days. Of course, between work sessions, we'd pause to taste the hospitality of the yacht club and town.

Simon's Town: Eclectic Navy Atmosphere

Simon's Town, South Africa, is located on a protected cove on False Bay that opens to the southeast in the direction of dominant summer winds. Winter, however, brings northwest winds and rain, making the Atlantic side of the peninsula and Cape Town very uncomfortable. Simon's Town provides a winter refuge for Cape Town citizens and becomes a summer playground in what has been called a quintessential English seaside town. It is considered a sheltered location that provides year-round protection for boats.

The town was named after Simon van der Stel who, as governor of the Cape Colony between 1677 and 1699, surveyed the bay and declared it a sheltered harbor for winter anchorage between May and September. The town became a royal naval base and in 1806, the home of the British South Atlantic Squadron. Admiral Lord Nelson was nursed through an illness on the first of his two visits to Simon's Town.

The modern naval breakwater and the Selborne Dry Dock were built in 1910. Over three hundred ships were repaired there during World War II while an estimated one hundred twenty-five Allied ships were sunk in bad weather, or by enemy action, near the town.

With independence achieved in 1956, the South African Navy took over the Simon's Town base. Today, it remains an important naval training and repair facility with huge updated stone moles that create a large sheltered naval harbor.

Three new South African stealth missile ships dominate the quay while a submarine and other small ships crowd around the dock. A large floating dry dock is moored next to the permanent Selborne Dry Dock facility. Surrounding repair shops and storage facilities fill the shipyard. The main access gate is just off Saint Georges Street.

Town sidewalks are filled with a mix of tourists and locals meeting and passing in the English left-hand style. At rush hour, pedestrian traffic is a potpourri of ethnicity, dominated by navy and shipyard personnel wearing a mixture of work clothes and fancy white Class-A uniforms. They walk with pride in their step, chatting among themselves and speaking to strangers. An occasional squad of recruits with full battle packs jogs toward a conditioning run on nearby mountain roads.

After dark, the sidewalks and streets are mostly abandoned. Over the wind, one can hear shipyard sounds, work whistles, clanks, and calls of workmen that continue round the clock.

"Wakie, wakie, rise and shine!" on a loudspeaker, starts the day with a laugh.

Simon's Town residences occupy the mountainside overlooking the bay. Beyond the main street, Cornwall Street, Thomas Lane, and Jackson Road snake along higher elevations where white stucco houses have colorful tile roofs and drifts of hanging flowery vines. Pedestrian alley stairs lead down the steep mountainside toward the town and bay.

Nineteenth-century colonial style connected buildings make a largely unbroken line for the entire mile-long length of the town. There are twenty-one attached buildings over one hundred fifty years old, each with a historic date plaque on the front door.

An intricate wrought-iron balustrade runs along the length of the covered sidewalk to separate patrons from angle parked cars and the road. They examine goods in gift shop windows while fully aware of the constant din of traffic. Several ATM machines on building fronts are sheltered from pedestrians by a thin plastic privacy shield.

Colorful facades provide clues to building use: the Central Hotel and British Hotel with their restaurants and balconies; garish psychedelic colored signs proclaiming cheap cell phones for sale; a storefront window, filled with grocery items and phone cards for sale; or more commonly, real estate *For Sale or Let* signs.

The center of town is dominated by historic Jubilee Square, a mini commons crowded with palm trees and cast iron lamps that illuminate the area around a bus and taxi stop. A tree-shaded cobblestone parking area fronts the single story façade of the Quayside Hotel. The hotel entrance opens to a well-decorated plaza with colorful flagpoles and 19th-century cannons pointing toward the harbor while its rear has four floors of rooms with balconies giving a terrific view of the bay.

A statue of Able Seaman Just Nuisance occupies a corner of the square. This dog, a Great Dane, was befriended by British naval personnel during WWII and was given the Able Seaman rank by the British Parliament. Sailors would say, "You're just a nuisance. Why do you have to lie here of all places?" The dog was born on April 30, 1937, enlisted on August 25, 1939, and died after being struck by a car on April 1, 1944. Just Nuisance, having befriended the naval personnel, was given a full military funeral and buried at a mountaintop signal station overlooking Simon's Town.

Artisan stalls fill small rental spaces on Jubilee Square with cheap African trinkets while nearby permanent shops feature large display windows of upscale merchandise. At the eastern corner of the park, a small farmer's market is open on Wednesday and Saturday. A historic ship's anchor monument is a hangout for lounging lads who survey the scene.

Near the bus stop, a small stone monument and bronze plaque remembers Apartheid with its exclusion of black citizens and harsh government action. The bronze plaque reads:

To the memory of generations of fellow citizens who dwelt here in peace and harmony until removed by the edict of 1967.

The message refers to Simon's Town designation as a white-only area by the Apartheid government. Coloured and black citizens were forced to leave their property and move to approved areas of the country.

To the east of Jubilee Square, down the cobblestone driveway is False Bay Yacht Club. A small parking area serves the club but also the Sea Rescue Facility, the Seven Seas Naval Officers Club, the Bronze Age Sculpture Gallery, the Warrior Toy Museum, and the Simon's Town Hall.

The Sea Rescue Facility (NSRI #10) is a unit of the National Sea Rescue Institution, which consists of twenty-one coastal stations and three inland stations. The NSRI has a staff of over eight hundred volunteers.

To the west and north of town, toward the village of Vishoek, are the utilitarian concrete town dock, the naval museum, the Simon's Town Museum, the Saint Francis of Assisi Church, the South African Navy Fleet Headquarters, a historic naval gun battery site, and the Metrorail station.

Bertha's, Dixie's, Penguin Point, Southern Right, Pescado, Black Marlin, Just Sushi, and Bon Appetite are a few restaurants sprinkled about town. Pubs named Trafalgar Bar, The Meeting Place, Harbor View, Fashionably Late, and Quarterdeck are prominent watering holes. These overpriced facilities fleece sailors and tourists alike.

Vehicles are driven on the left side of the road, British-style. Street signs are in English, but along Saint Georges Street are rather unique. A large penguin, enclosed in a red circle, warns motorist to watch for penguins on the road. Another road sign warns of an R500 fine for feeding wild baboons, while other signs have a large equal (=) to warn of approaching a crosswalk. Numbers in red circles are painted on the roadway to announce speed limits. A sign with a large colorful graphic describes the Southern Right Whale that is often seen swimming in False Bay.

When looking north from a higher elevation, one can see the churning bay water surrounding clearly marked Noah's Ark Rock and Roman Rocks. These shipping hazards have claimed numerous vessels.

The twin-hulled Blue Pointer, a commercial dive boat, is docked at FBYC. A three-foot-diameter cage, used for diver protection when shark diving, is prominently lashed to the bow along with a sign offering wreck-diving and shark-watching trips. Although diving visibility is often poor, the sandy bottom and shallow depths make an easy trip for experienced divers.

Simon's Town offers refuge for boats in the town anchorage, at the yacht club dock, or behind the navy yard mole. Local fishing boats are moored in the anchorage area near the large pipe frame where fishing nets are dried in the sun.

The unique quality of Simon's Town is understated elegance, with a naval atmosphere teeming with a mixture of young folk and tourists. I am impressed with its eclectic atmosphere.

James E. Keen

False Bay Yacht Club: Cruiser's Friend

A descending, winding cobblestone lane next to the farmer's market provides access to FBYC. A sliding barred security gate controls yacht club road traffic, while an adjacent pedestrian gate allows electronic key entry. Jean, the yacht club receptionist, indicates the gates are installed primarily to prevent tourists from wandering into the club facility but admits they also provide needed theft security.

The white stucco two-story, flat-roofed yacht club building shares a waterfront lot with the boatswain's shop (ship's store) and repair yard. A prominent concrete haul-out ramp used by a travel lift to remove boats from the bay for repair and storage is covered with rotting kelp that washes ashore with the six-foot ocean tide.

Bayside sliding glass doors adorn the front of the club and offer views of the docks, distant mountains, and seascape of False Bay. The first-floor patio has lounging chairs surrounded by colorful flowers while the second-floor full-width balcony holds straight back chairs used mainly by the smoking outcasts from the club bar.

A restaurant, toilet facilities, and Jean's office occupy the ground floor where she rules the area, keeping watch from her office overlooking the front gate and dock areas. She controls incoming and outgoing traffic with her electric lock switch and issues key disks to visiting sailors. A pleasure to talk with, Jean always has a comment about the weather or usual tips of where to find this or that.

Hanging behind Jean's desk are two pieces of artwork: a large oil painting of the Cape of Good Hope and an equally large photograph of Simon's Town taken from the bay, showing fire raging on the mountainside above the town. She explains that large non-native trees were planted and flourished on the dry hillsides and attracted frequent wildfires. A government program eliminated all non-native species allowing a return to natural semi-arid shrub that put an end to out-of-control wildfires.

Large, modern restroom facilities feature a gigantic white tile shower area with big, on-demand, propane-powered water heaters. Prominently posted signs remind guests to conserve water. However, we quickly learn, a hot shower is only assured after turning on at least two showers so that water demand is enough for the water heaters to

FBYC with Simon's Town in the background.

ignite.

A card-controlled, easy-to-use public telephone hangs from the wall outside the toilets. Telephone cards are common and can be bought from many locations for R20 (US $3.33) and other amounts. Calls are made by inserting the card and dialing. To place a call to the United States, you simply dial the country access code (091), the area code, and the telephone number. A five-minute call to the United States consumes an R20 card or about R3.50 (US$0.58) a minute.

The yacht club's second floor is a large playroom. A cloud of club burgees hangs from the decorative wood ceiling. Visitors have contributed their home club burgee so that the collection is truly international. A large bar area occupies the west end of the room where patrons lounge at all hours. At the back east corner is a television lounge and pool table area. The Bridge Office at the front east corner serves the club officers and offers a commanding view of the harbor. A mast on the balcony flies club colors and storm warning flags.

The bayside front yard has spotty, dry, walked-over brown grass with grazing pigeons. Outcrops of decorative boulders are sprinkled about the lawn while palm trees, large red flowering bushes, tables and colorful shade umbrellas adorn the rock paved patio area where potted plants provide additional color for restaurant patrons.

A whitewashed seawall holds back the sea and cradles the parched lawn where benches and lounging chairs are grouped for conversation. A barbecue grill completes the lawn ensemble.

The nearby False Bay Sea Rescue building crowds the east side of the club lawn where its bulk provides some shade for the grill and shelter from the constant southeasterly wind.

* * * * * *

A white handrail provides some security on the pedestrian bridge that leaps a span of perhaps fifty feet from the seawall to a large boulder in the bay. It springs lightly up and down with each step. Club floating docks are moored to the rock as are the dinghy landing and public floating dock area.

At the bay end of the bridge is a security gate where members and guests use their key disks to gain entry. Four floating docks form an E-shape with three arms that measure at least three hundred feet as they extend toward the east and the nearby mole of the navy yard.

Bill on the dock at False Bay Yacht Club

Sections of the docks are linked together to form moored floating modules, each about five feet wide by forty feet long. Modules are connected in a manner that leaves a six-inch void in the deck surface that presents a hazard that could result in a twisted or broken ankle.

Boats generally moor bow first to the pier, sometimes crowding the walkway with bowsprit gear, making the walk like negotiating an obstacle course. When walking down the pier, the view ahead is an undulating floating course of five-foot wide planks with obstacles surging into the walkway. When the frequent high wind is blowing, the moving pier truly becomes a hazard.

A lengthy floating breakwater shields the bay side of the club dock area and runs parallel to the shore with an opening near the western shoreline and another near the shipyard mole. High winds generate waves that crash over the breakwater and create a mist of spray that coats the docks with a drying seawater spray that leaves a fine powder of salt on everything.

Shipyard Mole with warships and odd clouds over the peninsular.

Residents along the dock are a mix of locals and visitors with some boats occupying a slip for extended periods. Most visiting boaters are sea gypsies who occupy the boat as their only home. Don and Mimi, from Texas, have lived on their boat for ten of the twenty-seven years that they have owned her. A German sailor displays huge pride in his floating home and will tell you about it with every visit. A singlehanded Norwegian sailor lives aboard an ancient wooden yawl.

"Boats become better the longer they are owned and sailed," Bill explains. "It takes a while to find a place to stow everything neatly but cruisers have the time to fix things up."

When we look at SA boats, we find that most are constructed of robust steel, demonstrating lessons learned from the tumultuous seas. Locals will tell you that fiberglass is for dinghies: proper boats are built of steel.

Advent II fits into that category—a proper boat of steel construction.

James E. Keen

Advent II: A Well Found Boat

Advent II has been owned by Bill and Normandie Doar since 1997. Both sailors have learned to handle her in all weather conditions and Bill has sailed her singlehandedly to the Caribbean and several times to Bermuda. Strongly built of steel, she is a well found thirty-six foot, hard-chined, utilitarian machine, absent of brightwork. Only necessary gear is aboard that is designed well and routinely duplicated for reliability.

It is important for the reader to know and understand the complexities and details of the boat while following our sea adventure. I have, therefore, described her with a fair amount of detail.

* * * * * *

She sits in a slip with each of her dock lines doubled, if not tripled as Bill wants to make sure everything stays attached to the dock. He does things for a reason, not just to make a statement or to appear proper.

White paint covers the steel construction of the vessel with small occasional bits of rust bleed where scratches have interrupted the protection. A wide dark blue painted wood rub railing runs the length of both topsides to provide a cushion from offending docks while a matching blue sail cover wraps around the boom. A heavy steel pipe cage surrounds the cockpit supporting a blue canvas cover underneath the solar panels and radar antenna that provides great shelter and protection for the helmsman.

The overall appearance of Advent II is a machine ready to take on the sea.

I climb over the starboard stainless steel lifelines, slipping past Normandie's windsurfing sailboard lashed there, to duck under steel tubing of the cockpit cage. It supports four fifty-five watt solar panels that provide two-hundred-twenty watts of solar power and the majority of the electric charge for the ship's batteries. Since we will always use the Global Positioning System (GPS) and Very High Frequency (VHF) radio while underway, use our computers routinely, and show running lights at night, the diesel engine will have to be run every five or six days to provide an additional boost to keep the batteries fully charged.

Twin manual stainless steel winches are located on each cockpit coaming and are used for controlling jib sheets and the mainsail preventer control line. Cockpit seat backs serve as a bulwark to partially deter errant sea spray that finds its way along the gunwale. Wide steel seats are coated with non-slip paint while a wooden slat seat cover provides comfort and dryness when the cockpit is wet.

The front of the cockpit forms a bridge deck that prevents seawater from making its way down the main companionway into the cabin. A sliding hatch cover and stout wooden hatch boards close the companionway during rough weather.

The steel cockpit foot well is about thirty inches wide and five feet long, with a removable slatted wooden floor. Twin drains carry seawater spray through the stern.

A fuzzy rope covering on the destroyer-style steering wheel is like short baggywrinkle on a line and is soft and warm on your hands on a cold night. The pedestal mounted wheel is at the aft end of the cockpit where the helmsman stands to steer or sits on the starboard seat to monitor the autopilot course. A binnacle steering compass is protected by a large helm guard of stainless tubing that also supports a holder for water bottles.

Engine controls are on the port side of the helm station. The broken gear shift lever has been satisfactorily replaced by locked-on vice grip pliers.

A three-foot wide, full-width wooden stern platform is mounted on sturdy pipe fittings and effectively makes the thirty-six foot boat into a thirty-nine foot boat for docking purposes. It provides a work area for servicing the self-steering wind vane, the outboard mounted main rudder, and the twin transom mounted propane tanks. The dinghy is boarded from the platform and while in port, we use the platform for swimming.

The self-steering device is a stern mounted WindPilot that Bill has affectionately named Windy. It has a lightweight but strong counterbalanced vertical wind vane and a folding shaft that extends downward into the water where a narrow auxiliary rudder assists in steering the boat.

A line and pulley system connect Windy to the helm. When underway, the helmsman steers a chosen course and then locks the steering lines to the helm. As the boat tacks or the wind changes direction, the vane is pushed down from vertical and that action turns the shaft to transmit the motion to the auxiliary rudder. The same motion is transmitted through the lines to the helm which corrects the ship's rudder and course. As the boat turns using both the main and auxiliary rudders, the wind vane regains its original upright position and the auxiliary rudder and helm return to a neutral position. Although rather complicated, the system is effective, powerful enough to steer the boat in heavy seas, and does not use electric power. An auxiliary electric autopilot is used while motoring.

The forward end of the cockpit has a dodger made of large diameter steel pipes wrapped in rubber tubing to prevent a nasty head knock. It has thick Plexiglas windows and a large area of covered coach roof that serves as a shelf for handy storage.

The slanted rear bulkhead of the main cabin cradles the electronic sailing instruments: wind speed/direction, boat speed, and GPS that is inoperative. A temporary bracket holds a handheld working GPS.

The portside lifeline provides a home for Shirley, a twelve foot, Porta Bote dinghy that folds neatly into compact panels for storage. The dinghy was named after Psalm 23:6: *Surely goodness and mercy shall follow me all the days of my life: and I will dwell in the house of the Lord forever*. Bill says it was their intent to choose Surely as the name of the dinghy; however, in keeping with the tradition of giving boats a female name, they chose the sound-alike Shirley. Goodness and Mercy are the names of a subsequent dinghy and runabout.

The dinghy outboard engine is stored outside on the port side stern railing while a yellow rigid man overboard throwing ring and rescue line pack are mounted inside. A lighted man overboard pole is fastened to the portside vertical cockpit roof support.

Several short small diameter lanyards with neatly whipped ends are tied to the port side lifeline. We find them handy for lashing equipment in place.

A one-gallon garden sprayer is secured to the rear corner of the cockpit. Daily cockpit baths using warm fresh water rinses from this clever device are a luxury.

* * * * * *

Twin walkways, each about thirty inches wide, lead forward along the starboard and port lifelines. A heavy steel safety cable runs along each walkway to be used as a connection for your personal safety tether when going forward but tends to roll awkwardly under your feet. Bill requires that the safety harness and inflatable life vest be worn at all times on deck while at sea. In addition, one of the two personal harness tethers will be attached to a safe hard point at all times.

Amidships and forward of the dodger is the wide coachroof coated with white non-slip paint and twin gray, sun-bleached teak handrails along both sides of its length. A six-man emergency inflatable life raft and the main cabin ventilation hatch occupy the area aft of the mast.

Fashioned like tripods of stainless pipe, a pair of granny bars bracket the mast to protect cabin vents from errant footsteps but are tall enough to provide a secure bracing and safety tie off point so that both hands can be used to work the mast mounted winches.

The aluminum mast has twin backstays, twin amidships stays, and a stout forestay where the twin roller furling gear is mounted. The backstays have insulators that isolate wire sections for use as the antenna for the ship's SSB radio. Two large winches mounted at the base of the mast are used to control the halyards for the mainsail, twin jibs, and topping lifts.

A fiberglass hatch covers the emergency exit from the forward cabin and provides deck access to the forward sail locker. A stainless steel solar powered ventilator penetrates the hatch to provide some air circulation below when the hatch is closed.

Plastic water jugs are lashed to the port lifelines opposite the mast while diesel jugs are mirrored on the starboard. These containers store emergency supplies; however, their primary use is to transport fuel and water from shore sources. A canvas cover is lashed over the jugs to slow the deteriorating effects of UV rays.

A large spare plow-style anchor lashed along the port gunwale aft of the water jugs is a painful toe catcher.

Twin roller furling rigs are mounted on the headstay so that two jibs can be flown or furled at the same time. The huge genoa jibs are easily deployed or stowed by simply pulling or releasing a line from the cockpit. It's a huge blessing to deploy the jibs from the cockpit rather than having to go forward to manually hank-on or corral a wildly flogging sail.

This twin headsail arrangement, called flying wing-n-wing when both sails are flying, will be used often and provide the major propulsion for the boat. Light but stout poles connect the mast and the outside corner of the jib when deployed. Holding the sail out from the boat with the horizontally mounted pole gives a big boost in sail efficiency. Launching and retrieving these poles will comprise most of the forward deck work while underway.

A one-hundred-ten pound plow-style main anchor is snubbed on a roller and dangles over the bow where it is secured by a capture pin and a safety lanyard. A stout chain anchor rode, four hundred feet in length, runs back to a manual windlass, then down into the chain locker. My duties will include winching in the chain rode and heavy anchor.

* * * * * *

To gain access to the companionway and accommodations below, a giant step is required to climb over the bridge deck. I find it easier to stand on the cockpit seat, duck under the dodger, turn aft, and climb down the four-step ladder to the cabin sole.

The utilitarian wooden sole (floor) is fitted with numerous bilge hatches for stored fuel, water, food, and gear and are secured by safety latches to prevent disgorging their contents in case of a knockdown.

The small engine room located behind the companionway ladder and below the cockpit floor is adjacent to the Captain's cabin. It houses the boat's diesel engine—a marinized diesel tractor engine.

Moving forward, the curtained door to the Captain's cabin is to port. The tiny cabin is mostly a narrow bed but does have a tiny floor space—about three square feet.

On the starboard of the main cabin is an aft-facing navigation and radio station located in a cubby under the starboard forward cockpit seats. The single sideband radio will be our voice contact with the world and the mode of sending and receiving emails. The ship's computer and other electronic gear are sheltered here while the radar screen is mounted on a swivel arm that pivots to the center of the companionway directly in the helmsman's view from the cockpit.

Forward, along the starboard hull of the cabin in the area meant to be used as a pilot berth is a large ice chest used for miscellaneous storage. We do not have refrigeration and will only bring ice aboard while in port to cool our sundowner drinks.

On the port side, forward of the Captain's cabin, is a fore and aft bulkhead that is the back side of the head (toilet) but the entrance is located around the corner in the galley area. Virginia, the composting toilet is installed here. With each use, she requires the addition of a handful of organic material to aid decomposition. She and I never got well acquainted as I mostly avoided her. While at sea, we use a very utilitarian bucket in the cockpit.

Bill says, "The bucket is easier to use and clean; get over it."

A counter runs across the center of the main cabin in order to place the galley sink on the centerline so that it will drain on either tack. The cook works facing aft at the sink or facing toward the galley stove mounted on the port side hull where a generous fresh food hammock and larder also lives.

Overhead wooden handholds provide hard point security while at sea. When walking about during rough weather, it is a matter of grabbing one overhead handhold after another to maintain balance for the trip across the cabin.

The ship's bell has a dangling lanyard, made of a custom knotted line. The time and effort used to tie and braid the line is an example of the art of sailcraft that Bill practices. The bell is mounted on the head bulkhead near the galley sink.

Advent II's cook stove is a Force 10, three-burner propane model. It has a gimbaled mounting so pots stay level while at sea and stainless wire fiddles that hold pots in place over the burners. Bill has installed a simple cutoff switch and a timer switch for the propane feed in addition to the usual control knobs for each burner. If you forget to turn off the burner, the timer will automatically turn it off after a brief period. The switches are a necessary safety addition. However, to use the stove for long periods, like baking bread, you have to remember to periodically reset the timer.

Forward of the galley sink and starboard of the mast is a folding galley table with low edge fiddles to keep plates and utensils from crashing to the sole. A cushioned salon bench along the starboard hull is seating for eating, lounging, or more frequently, using my laptop. A kerosene cabin heater on the opposite side of the galley table will not be used for this summer voyage. At the head of the table on a polished wooden bulkhead is a large decorative brass antique, fully functional ship's running lamp. Photos, just snapshots taped to the wall, show highlights of the circumnavigation—pictures of Bill and Normandie in the Pacific.

Suspended over the galley table is a large blow-up vinyl world globe. We frequently use it to find a location to make a point in our wide-ranging discussions.

My accommodations occupy all the space forward of the mast. Through a curtained doorway is a people clean-up area with a sink, a locker for toothpaste and stuff, a folded clothes locker, and a hanging clothes rack. Forward of that is the forepeak sail locker where sails, travel bags, plastic bags of paper goods (toilet tissue, etc.), deck chairs, and miscellaneous things live.

Along the starboard side of the space is my bunk. It is about thirty inches wide at the head and four feet wide at the foot. The smaller space allows my head to be held tightly so that I don't flop around in the seaway.

A big wooden panel stores vertically to separate the bunk from the passageway. When I want to have a double berth, I fold the wood panel down into the passageway to make a huge berth almost the size of a king-sized bed. In my single bunk configuration, the big mattress is stored underneath and up the side of the hull.

The sails for Normandie's windsurfer live above my bunk, suspended from an overhead rack. These large bundles fill the overhead with cloth and make my sleeping area cave-like. It will be a great place to wedge my clock so I can easily see the time.

These very adequate accommodations are larger than the Captain's small, coffin-like cabin.

I am pleased with the boat. She is well-used, sturdy, and sufficient. Advent II is certainly an adequate sailing machine for the task ahead.

I am anxious to begin my first blue-water ocean crossing.

James E. Keen

Monday, Jan 10, 2005

Boulders Beach and Cape Point National Park

James Doonan arrives in his Rikkis to take us to the Cape of Good Hope Nature Reserve and Cape Point Lighthouse.

"Morning," he says. "I've got a couple of friends to share the trip and expenses."

Unloading the Rikkis at Boulders Beach.

Three tourists are seated in the two small back seats making six people total for the minivan taxi. James politely asks me to sit in front, leaving Bill to share the back seats. A Dutch couple is scrunched on the rear seat while Bill sits with an English lad. After introductions, we speed off to our first stop.

* * * * * *

Boulders Beach, a protected part of Table Mountain National Park, is crowded on the seashore by a residential area. James tells us that this beach is the home of a breeding colony of African Penguins.

A South African Penguin hides from bathers.

At the edge of the parking lot, we scramble onto one of the many house-sized boulders that litter the beach. Sea surf swells around the rock leaving sand swirls for the next wave to reshape. With not a penguin in sight, James suggests that today they may have moved down the beach.

Bill points to a bush and yells, "Penguin Ahoy!"

The tiny, twenty-four inch high, black docile creature stands shivering with fright or cold. It is very different from the familiar TV penguins that are at least four-feet tall and look like they are suited in a tuxedo.

James tells us that penguins are flightless birds that usually inhabit southern ocean climates from Antarctica to the Galapagos Islands. African Penguins inhabit only the African continent and offshore islands where breeding populations, estimated at one and a half million

Bathers enjoy swimming among boulders.

in 1910 have been reduced by the harvesting of eggs to just over one million today. Known for their donkey-like braying cry, the penguin was formerly named the Jackass Penguin but changed today to be more politically correct.

Scattered among the bushes are other penguins that appear unafraid of humans although they will not let us approach. After admiring these diminutive creatures, we walk down the beach to admire bikini-clad ladies.

* * * * * *

Back aboard the minibus, the road snakes around sharp mountain outcrops as we ride past Bellows Rock, Anvil Rock, and Dias Rock beaches, each named for their wild rock formations that sweep into the sea.

At Dias Rock, a huge stone cross honoring the famous navigator Bartolomeu Dias has been erected as a navigational beacon while less than a mile away, the Da Gama cross lives higher up the mountainside. When the two crosses are lined up from the sea for navigation, they point toward Whittle Rock, a large submerged shipping hazard out in False Bay.

We enter Cape Point National Park, paying our fees and receiving a warning about feeding or approaching the aggressive Chacma baboons, ostrich, or elk-like creatures in the park.

This end of the peninsula consists of three mountains. Cape Point Mountain is the easternmost, with Cape MaClear Mountain in the middle, and Cape of Good Hope Mountain on the west. These mountains form a fishtail-like land feature at the southwestern end of Africa.

A short ride takes us to the parking area for the Cape Point Lighthouse. We unfold from the minibus, cross the parking lot, and queue up to board the Flying Dutchman Funicular Railway. Two small modern railroad cars are counterbalanced on either end of a single cable with one car going up the single track while the other comes down. Just as the cars are about to crash in the middle, a second track diverts one car, and the two cars safely pass.

The unusual looking railroad cars have an undercarriage that somewhat levels the steep climb or descent of the tracks. Large

Funicular Railroad cars with slanted floors.

windows at the front and rear offer a panoramic view while side windows are slanted so as to become somewhat level while going up or down. Passengers sit facing the rear at different levels on the sloped floor with each seat affording a magnificent view of the Indian and Atlantic Oceans on opposite sides of the car and the peninsula.

At the top of the railroad ride, an arduous climb up stone steps takes us to a massive black steel lighthouse cylinder. It's only about twenty feet tall and perched on a rock outcrop at the top of Cape Point Mountain. It is topped with large windows that surround the light while a stone walkway with protecting wall surrounds the lighthouse where spectators ogle incredible views from the tallest sea cliffs in South Africa. It is an eight-hundred-sixteen-foot look down to rocks and crashing surf below.

Stone steps leading to Cape Point Lighthouse.

Cape Point was identified by Dias in 1488 but the first lighthouse was not built until 1860. Because of its lofty height, the light was often obscured by fog, rendering it useless. A second light was built on a lower perch at nearby Dias Lookout Point and is today the most powerful light in South Africa. Modern ships depend on radar and GPS navigation for safety; however, illuminated lighthouses within sight of each other are still maintained.

View of sea from Cape Point Lighthouse, where Advent II sailed past a few days later.

The 360-degree view offers magnificent vistas of the two oceans and the eastern peninsula coastline almost all the way back to Simon's Town. A direction pole tells us New York City is 7,000 miles in a northwesterly direction.

James had told us earlier that the warm Agulhas Current originates in the Indian Ocean while the Atlantic Ocean Benguela Current is much cooler as it originates near the Antarctic. When these currents meet off Cape Point, with a large temperature difference, the result is a violent clash just where Advent II will pass in a few days. Diaz originally named the Cape of Good Hope with a more menacing name—The Cape of Storms.

Cape Point Lighthouse sign gives world distances.

I stand and look at the ocean horizon and feel the energy and magic. It's a place of legends, just like our familiar Graveyard of the Atlantic off North Carolina's Cape Hatteras.

The Flying Dutchman, made famous in 17th-century nautical folklore, foundered while rounding this cape in heavy weather. The ship's Captain vowed that he would round the cape if it took him until doomsday to do so. The well-known legend sparked sightings of ghost ships throughout the world but the most common sightings are off the shores of Africa. Over the years, usually in bad weather, the Flying Dutchman is reported trying to round the cape.

Another famous shipwreck, in April 1911, took place at midnight in thick fog. The Portuguese luxury liner Lusitania (not the British Lusitania sunk by German subs on May 6, 1915) struck Bellows Rock just a few miles west of the cape. The well-known incident became the principal reason for rebuilding the defunct lighthouse at Cape Point.

Other historic shipwrecks that litter the nearby coastline include the Kakopoa, a steamship that foundered in 1900. The wreck is easily accessible on the western peninsula beach at nearby Sunset Beach Guest House.

We have a much easier walk down hill and ride back to the parking area where we join James in the minibus for the short trip over to the Cape of Good Hope beach.

* * * * * *

Along the road, a colony of Chacma baboons causes a traffic jam. This is the only protected troop of this rare species in Africa. Their diet consists of insects, scorpions, fruit, roots, and honey and during low tide, they can be seen roaming the beach feeding on shellfish and sand hoppers. The baboons are dangerous to humans, so people stay in their cars.

We drive past a Bontebok antelope with a new foal. These antelopes are the rarest in South Africa with a herd of a little over eight hundred in the wild from a low count of eighty-four animals in 1931.

A little farther on, we see a Cape Point Ostrich as it runs down the beach.

* * * * * *

A sign proclaims Cape of Good Hope to be the southwestern most point of Africa. James and Bill quickly point out that Cape Agulhas, about one hundred miles to the east where Bill and Normandie sailed past a few weeks earlier, is the actual southernmost point of the continent. However, they do concede, after an argument about semantics, that Cape of Good Hope is the southwestern most point of the continent.

Bill climbs a rocky hill for a better view while most of us remain in the parking lot. On his stumbling retreat down a switchback trail, he encounters the Dassie or Rock Hyrax. This small furry mammal looks like an oversized guinea pig or rabbit with rounded ears and no tail. It has large fang-like teeth that are little used as they prefer their molars to chew grass and other woody foods. Four stumpy toes on each front foot, with three toes on each rear foot, all have a rubbery bottom texture to aid in rock climbing. This mixed-up creature is a relative of the elephant but looks like it was designed by a committee of drunken sailors.

For the remainder of our guided tour, we engage our international companions in conversation while riding over mountain passes toward home. We arrive at Simon's Town to end a lovely outing and in time to find lunch.

* * * * * *

Bill introduces me to two great places on Saint Georges Street: a storefront bakery serving fresh bread and sweets, and in a back alley, the Homemade Shop that is like a convenience store back home. Fresh salads, meat pies, lasagna, and more bread are available at the shop and look truly homemade. We buy freshly prepared dishes and take them back to the boat to eat half for lunch and save the other half for dinner.

* * * * * *

My first duty aboard Advent II is to empty all the food lockers and make a list of the existing food. This has to be done before we restock the larder. On my hands and knees, I open the fifteen or so bilge lockers and pull the naked cans out onto the sole.

Labels have been removed from the cans to prevent insect infestation. Deciphering PCH AU (peaches from Australia) and other cryptic symbols written with black marker pen on the can tops is a challenge. I complete the Excel spreadsheet inventory and earn a "Well done!" from the Captain.

At sundown, with the wind blowing forty-five knots, we have a hot shower, dinner of leftover salad and a meat pie, and then a casual two-hour conversation.

At 2300 hours, Bill brings the night to a close by saying, "I'm two hours late for my bunk!"

I sit at my computer writing my personal log and thinking about tomorrow's shopping trip and the problems that the high winds may cause as we move the boat to the town fuel dock.

I'm beginning to feel more confident around Bill. He's affable, agreeable, intelligent, and full of interesting tidbits that he liberally shares. We have carved out our roles; one of master and pupil. He is leery of my unfamiliarity with the surroundings but tolerant of my inexperience. I try to keep a low profile and not antagonize him while I learn. It's a tactic that I hope will be rewarded by a successful relationship. I am beginning to understand some of the huge pressure he shoulders in getting the boat ready for sea.

When I climb into my bunk, I notice the wind has stopped. I think how it would be great to start towards home tomorrow. However, there are many more departure chores to be accomplished before we put to sea.

Getting Serious about Voyage Preparations

Bill is a list maker. On the first list of needs: diesel fuel, diesel oil filters, groceries for sixty days, fresh water, propane, and a six-volt battery for a safety light. In addition, the Captain needs to officially check me in as a crew member with Customs and then check Advent II out of the country for our departure scheduled on Thursday or Friday.

Our first stop is an auto parts store near the village of Fish Hook; no joy on the elusive oil filter. The problem is that the boat's Vetus diesel was originally manufactured as a Dutch farm tractor engine and in South Africa's semi-arid climate, farming tractor engine oil filters are not needed. The fact that the engine is old complicates the search.

The second stop is the camping store next door that does not have the needed battery.

The third stop is the Pick-N-Pay grocery store. It is similar to its stateside counterpart, with wide brightly-lit aisles, shelves filled with canned and boxed food, a large produce section, a bakery, and other specialty shops.

We are amazed at the large selection of usual and unusual produce. Into the cart go fresh whole pineapples, apples, oranges, and bananas. I find familiar products that have a definite British influence. Goods are packaged much differently, but the content labels are largely the same as in the US. In an hour, we overfill two carts with fruit, canned goods, and fresh artisan bread.

At the yacht club parking lot, we have the task of hauling all of those tiny plastic grocery bags through security gates and down the long floating dock to our boat, without getting blown off the pier. We are wet with salt water spray when we finish.

While Bill creates more lists and makes a telephone call to arrange for buying diesel fuel, I again remove all the old food items from the bilge food lockers, remove labels from new items, mark and stow them, piling old food cans on top of the new. Some old cans are getting rusty so I place them in a plastic milk crate lashed to the top of the galley table to be used first. The new groceries are entered on my food spreadsheet so that I now have a good idea of what we have and where everything is located.

* * * * * *

Bill tells me that the fuel man will meet us at 1500 hours. We have to stow everything securely before we can move the boat over to the fuel dock. The wind is blowing at thirty knots.

Bill coaches me through the diesel start-up and the engine roars reassuringly. On the foredeck, we have a dry run on how we will back out of the slip, motor around the end of the dock, and motor down the fairway between lines of docked boats to reach the fuel dock. My role includes tossing off the lines, standing lookout, and fending off and tying lines at the fuel dock. We get underway and reach the fuel dock without damage.

It takes sixty-seven U.S. gallons to top off Advent II's tanks. The fuel man is pleasant as we talk about the price of diesel (four dollars a gallon), the weather, other trivia, and then return to our slip without incident.

In the afternoon, I talk to Louise, the financial secretary of FBYC, about hanging my Cypress Landing Yacht Club burgee from the ceiling of their bar area where many other visiting club burgees are displayed.

"No problem, sir! I'll hang it right away," she replies with a cheerful smile.

Cypress Landing Yacht Club Burgee hanging from ceiling of False Bay Yacht Club in Simon's Town, South Africa (R).

After dinner, the other half of lunch, and a shower, we go for a beer at the FBYC bar. My CLYC burgee is proudly flying from the ceiling among a gaggle of burgees from around the world. I take pictures to show my club friends back home.

Meeting up with a local sailor from the docks, I have to lightly defend the iris design on my club burgee. His comments, along with comments of other sailors at the bar are not too friendly. Other clubs have very masculine boat related symbols on their flags to show strength or courage. Our neighborhood flag features an iris logo, so our yacht club adopted the same logo. The teasing comments are in jest and we all have a good laugh.

A sailor's parting shot is, "It's rather pretty, mate!"

43

Wednesday, Jan 12, 2005

Official Paperwork, Exploring Cape Town, and Table Mountain

To check me into the country as a crew member of Advent II and announce our intent to depart requires traveling by train up the bay to Cape Town. The Simon's Town Metrorail station is a modern stone building with a sturdy appearance. A lengthy concrete concourse runs along the railroad tracks beside the bay. Windswept waves crash ashore east of the tracks for much of the ride north to Cape Town.

The sturdy South African electric train service is fast and economical.

The Metrorail features modern red trains, very substantially built, as are most things in South Africa. An R25 ticket buys a pleasant seventy minute local ride with twenty-six quick stops. Passengers boarding and departing at each stop are a mixture of races and social stations. At one point, I decide a university must be near as young adults carry backpacks board. At another stop, several youngsters are dressed in school uniforms and get off near a high school.

Modern Cape Town with Table Mountain in the background.

I enjoy prudently profiling people. Although we are wary of danger, the ride has a safe feel even while two police officers ride each railcar and are prominent at the stations.

Our route follows the shoreline through Muizenberg where the tracks turn northward, curving around Table Mountain, to arrive at the main Cape Town train station. At a wide enclosed platform, people rush towards an exit and we are engulfed in the crowd as it flows out onto the street.

Wide avenues among a forest of high-rise office buildings offer vistas of Table Mountain and the shimmering blue harbor between buildings to the north. From the train station, a short walk takes us to the immigration office. I am added to the crew list of Advent II. Our outbound clearance to the U.S. is immediately filed—to be executed within a reasonable time, as weather permits.

The customs office, the same one that requires me to have a return airline ticket in order to enter the country, blesses our departure. That eight hundred dollar second half of my plane ticket will become an expensive souvenir.

With our chores now complete, it is time to play.

* * * * * *

At the Royal Cape Yacht Club (RCYC), a huge banner is displayed, advertising their America's Cup participation in 2007. The white stucco club building is scrunched between a major railroad yard and the harbor. Long lines of rail cars, carrying freight that has been unloaded from ships, are parked in the yard while another lengthy train rumbles past.

Specialized trucks, loaded with seagoing freight containers, roar past the club entrance. The club building is separated from this noisy chaos by a small parking area.

Inside, the club is calm and inviting. A classy lady at the front desk gives us a cordial welcome and invites us to enjoy the yacht club facilities. Famous and not-so-famous, sailors have traditionally made the RCYC their home while in Cape Town. At the richly decorated bar, stocked with two bartenders and a mirror wall that displays brightly colored bottles, we choose a glass of water. Although the bar is cool and inviting, we go to the veranda overlooking the harbor where we bask in the warm sun while catching our breath from the lengthy walk from downtown.

Bill in front of the Royal Cape Yacht Club, Cape Town, South Africa.

Bill surveys the club docks for familiar boats while I photograph the club harbor with rows of docks where member boats, mostly sailboats, rest in assigned slips. A rock jetty separates the club harbor from the commercial harbor and the ocean bay on the horizon.

We stroll out to the visitor docks. Bill finds familiar boats and two acquaintances from former ports of call. After I am introduced, Bill and his friends get caught up on cruisers' news. They speak with the assurance of seasoned sailors swapping stories of adventures past. I listen in awe.

Moving down the dock, we locate the sailboat Adventura III. Owned by Jimmy Cornell, this boat and others has been featured in many of his books about cruising, including the popular World Cruising Routes, World Cruising Destinations, and World Cruising Handbook. The boat is unoccupied and we are unable to meet the famous author, cruiser, adventurer, and organizer of worldwide sailing rallies.

Back in the club, I use a computer to send quick email messages and then purchase a baseball cap and RCYC burgee to start my collection. I leave my CLYC burgee at the RCYC. I hope they will display it promptly like Louise did back at FBYC. I now have two burgees in my growing collection.

* * * * * *

At Table Mountain Cableway Station, we take a ride to the top of the famous flat-topped mountain in a huge sixty-five passenger round cable car. It has a rotating floor, giving each person an equal view of the scenery. Each car weighs eleven thousand pounds, weighted with water

ballast for stability in the frequent strong winds. The weather is calm today and the cloudless sky reminds me of beautiful Carolina Blue skies back home.

Orographic clouds, generated by upwelling air, periodically obscure the flat top mountain with white clouds, like a table cloth. But not today! Riding up the

Unique cable car at Table Mountain.

almost vertical cliff of the mountain side, the round blue rotating cable car offers us a clear view of Cape Town, the harbor, and the Atlantic Ocean.

48

At the mountain top, a cable car station is constructed of rock. It sits on the edge of the cliff; the only blemish on the flat featureless mountaintop surface of solid exposed pale pink rock. Rock walls at the edge of the overlook protect the crowd that is vying for a view through the telescopes.

Warnings signs and guidelines painted on the ground alert visitors to the danger of getting too close to the sheer cliffs.

Visitors enjoying a special view and great day.

Below, Cape Town sprawls north to the harbor and east to a rolling plain before a mountain range. Lush vineyards are in sight north of the city. Robben Island, the island prison where Nelson Mandela was kept, is a lump in the northwest Atlantic. I can see ships making their approach to the harbor.

Below is Lion's Head Mountain, covered by the rich indigenous cape vegetation called Fynbos, the unusual name of some eight thousand five hundred species of Cape Coral Kingdom plants. The national park supports these species, along with a variety of small animals, in the semi-arid terrain. Many of the plants are unique and cannot be found elsewhere in the world. The mountain has an angular rock craggy peak summit that sits atop a green mountain cone.

Devil's Head Mountain, a similar rugged stratified bulk, is to the east. From Table Mountain, at the northern end of the mountain range forming the Cape Peninsula, the look south is crowded with numerous mountain peaks that march south to Cape Point.

On our descent, the rotating car gives alternating panoramic views of the city and the sheer cliff face of the mountain.

* * * * * *

We leave the mountain and travel downtown to visit The Pie Stop, a small square tin-roofed building adorned with advertising signs and

graffiti. Much as the hamburger is a national favorite in the United States, South Africa favors round meat pies. The snack contains an unrecognizable, but tasty, filling inside a round golden textured crust. It is a sufficient meal and eating fried meat pies while sitting on a tree lined square, seems to be

Bill Doar at Fried Pie Shop in downtown Cape Town, South Africa

popular. We watch Cape Town residents scurry about as we eat.

On the return walk toward the train station, a shabby, thin, and sick looking black lady with an infant on her arm is panhandling. I'm instantly alert and uncomfortable but Bill displays a compassionate gaze and engages her in quiet conversation. After giving her some bills, he comments about how fortunate we are. She smiles at his words and that is all the thanks Bill needs.

* * * * * *

Back in Simon's Town, we buy more fresh fruit at the farmers' market to add to the larder. Bill makes some phone calls while I top off the water tanks as maybe my last chore before leaving port.

Thursday, Jan 13, 2005

More Preparations for Sailing

Almost like turning a switch, the wind stops and it's a wonderfully clear seventy-five degree day. However, we can't get underway until all our chores are completed.

Bill puts on his wetsuit and jumps into the clear seawater to inspect Advent II's hull. I stand safety watch, ready to sound the alarm if I see a shark or one of the aggressive seals that we have seen sunning themselves on the docks.

The propeller is clear of barnacles. However, weed grows everywhere on the wide flat steel bottom, while the waterline trails slimy weedy tendrils. Even with antifouling bottom paint, anything that gets wet with regularity grows a soft slimy unsightly weed. Bill says it doesn't affect boat speed, however, pride in a well-kept boat keeps him swimming around the waterline, scraping off the weed. It floats around the boat like hair on the floor of a barbershop.

"Well done!" he announces.

* * * * * *

At noon, the wind is blowing hard again as we walk east on Saint Georges Street to the Old Town Cemetery. It's located up the mountain slope at a picturesque site overlooking the bay.

Two sections of the cemetery are divided by a center walkway. The west side is a forest of ancient tombstones laying in disrepair among overgrown arid vegetation. The east side has been renovated by removing the old headstones and pouring decorative concrete. The old tombstones have been used to create large common memorial structures.

We read about 20th Century ships lost at sea, feeling the agony of the AB (Able-Bodied Seaman) who "fell from aloft on September 9, 1848." One memorial lists ordinary seaman, along with the Commander of the Fleet, on a single monument. We marvel at putting titles aside, honoring men together in a fight against their common foe, the sea.

Bill inspecting renovated tombstones at Simon's Town Cemetery.

At the top of the cemetery, we turn to admire the naval shipyard below, the town just to the west behind the hill and trees, the bay to the north beyond the shipyard, and the blue expanse of False Bay on the eastern horizon. What a gorgeous view on this hot blustery day.

On our stroll down a hillside residential street, we look at neat white masonry houses with colorful tile roofs and functional security shutters.

A dog challenges our intrusion as we walk carefully down the steep stairs leading directly to Saint Georges Street.

Our morning excursion is delightful.

* * * * * *

In the afternoon, Bill sends me to find a propane bottle that he had sent to Vishoek to be refilled. I call for a Rikkis and our old friend James collects me.

"Where did you leave it?" he queries.

"A yachtie from the docks took it to town for us. He's not returned, so I don't know where. That's your job!"

James stops at the petrol store and calls several propane shops. He comes out after a moment, a smile on his face, saying he has located the tank. We ride north on the M4 bayside road.

On our return, James stops at the train station to pick up five tourists fares. They wedge into the back and we find ourselves chatting about Boulders Beach and The Cape of Good Hope Nature Reserve.

I recommend James as a tour guide.

* * * * * *

With our preparations almost complete, Bill's plan to get underway is to move the boat to the open sea anchorage beyond the protective floating sea wall, stow all the loose deck gear, rig the topping lifts and poles, and secure the boat for sea. We will begin our watch standing routine and when appropriate, raise the anchor and sail away.

But, our actions depend on an acceptable level of wind. By the time I get back to the docks, masts are howling in a thirty-five knot blow. We can't move the boat to the anchorage in this wind.

* * * * * *

At nightfall, we go to the club bar, sitting on the smoker's balcony, away from the crowd noise. There are few smokers and the cool night air and sounds of the sea are nice. A Norwegian sailor friend from the dock sits with us. He has sailed from his home, across the Atlantic to the Caribbean, down to Brazil, and then back across the Atlantic to South Africa. He is sailing an old wooden yawl, a gift from his sailing parents and his home as a kid. We can see his red-hulled boat on the hard in the yard, the wooden bottom and sides coated with painted fiberglass. He has hauled her for routine maintenance before continuing his trip. The boat has the latest electronic toys aboard but remains otherwise a classic.

We discuss the satellite weather chart our friend had received that afternoon. It suggests we should stay another day, possibly another week, until the southwestern winds become northwestern winds, and then back around to the normal southeastern wind pattern. Southeastern winds will blow us home, while northwestern winds would blow us back onto the African continent from the stormy Atlantic. We may have to enjoy another day of hot showers, fresh bread, and cold beer.

Well darn, trapped in paradise!

Friday, Jan 14, 2005

Bill sends me on yet another attempt to find oil filters and the elusive six-volt battery. We'd tried several times to find both items, but with new information about the filter, I take a Rikkis back to the Midas Store at the Long Beach Shopping Center. Armed with a sample filter and new part number, the clerk gives a no joy. He then notices another part number on the sample filter.

He looks up that number and beams, "I've got eleven of those, Mate!"

With a precision caliper that Bill had supplied, I measure the seal area, the diameter, and note that the height of the filter is not the same.

"No problem, Mate," the counter man says. "It will just hold more oil and be better."

With a usable filter in hand, I buy six. Another list item has been accomplished.

* * * * * *

The SSB radio has spotty reception while docked and is limited in sending lengthy messages. The uploading of digital photos via SSB is out of the question, being too slow and using too much of our allowed air time. At an internet store, Bill uploads trip pictures to his website while I catch up on personal email.

At the Homemade Store, we select the salad plate and a meat pie for lunch and sit in an outdoor dining area. A shade tree shelters three plastic dining tables in the fifteen foot wide alley paved with stone blocks. The tablecloths are sparking clean as is the delightfully cool alley on the windy seventy five degree afternoon. In the sheltered alley, howling wind is only a quiet whisper.

Our salad plate has big-chunk potato salad, a colorful bean salad, and refreshing coleslaw. Combined with a hot meat pie, Coke for Bill, and water for me, we dine!

* * * * * *

My baseball cap was on my head when I arrived on Sunday but has been eaten by Advent II. I've looked for it all week, peeking into lockers that may have gobbled it. One must avoid going without a hat as the strong overhead sun will cook exposed skin in short order.

My spare hat is a floppy Gilligan's Island-style beanie that I bought last year at the Juneau, Alaska Macaulay Salmon Hatchery. With no other hat available, I put on the goofy thing and have worn it all week.

Here is this big fat guy with white hair and beard, khaki shorts, big fat knees, short-sleeve shirt, sandals, sunglasses, and a goofy hat. All this time, I have been thinking that people were staring because I'm American. Now, I'm thinking it must be the hat. I've got to find that baseball cap.

* * * * * *

"It's still happy hour!" Bill announces.

A rare Friday night business meeting causes overcrowding at the yacht club bar as I wade through bodies to order Castle Beer. We retire to the balcony to escape the din but find ourselves among a thick group of ostracized smokers. The smoke is noxious, however, it's more tolerable than the packed crowd inside.

A well-preserved older lady comes over to meet the Americans. She introduces herself as a California girl that married a South African man. She lives in Zambia but makes her holiday at Simon's Town on her motor yacht named Miss Pickles.

"Tonight was special," she purrs. "I've been coming to this club for dozens of years, however, tonight I became a full club member." The club only recently started admitting women, so she was among the first to be inducted.

She tells us about living on a working farm in Zambia and how she escapes for holiday, as many South Africans do, to Simon's Town. The conversation turns to food. I suspect she is fishing for an invitation to join us at the club restaurant. We talk about our boats and then about cooking aboard tonight. I ask her about her choice of food aboard.

"Heavens, I don't cook!" was her terse reply.

After a few more minutes of polite conversation, Bill and I make our excuses and go back to the boat. We enjoy a luxurious hot shower, eat leftover supper aboard, and go to bed.

Saturday, Jan 15, 2005

It's still blowing hard! As I stare at the wind speed indicator, it hovers near twenty knots before jumping to thirty knots. Bill says the instrument uses a five-second averaging period, so the indicated wind is real—not just highest gust. Yesterday, we missed our departure because the weather forecast called for high winds off Cape Point.

"It's not known as the Cape of Storms for nothing," was the tired comment of a local at the club bar last night.

We putter around the boat most of the morning with Bill talking to friends on the SSB and listening to the Cruiser's Net for news and a weather report.

* * * * * *

I clean and repair the topside main cabin ventilation hatch. The job requires that I ream holes in two stainless brackets to install larger bolts. Bill finds the electric drill, a metal cutting bit, and C-clamps while I lay out an electrical extension cord. I plug it into an onboard electrical inverter that converts twelve-volt battery power into U.S. standard one-hundred-twenty-volt AC current. We're not using the shore power connection on the dock with its nonstandard two-hundred-forty-volts and receptacles that will not fit our shore power cables. We rely on the boat solar panels, big battery bank, and onboard inverter for our power needs.

I tie a lanyard to each steel bracket and the bitter end to my belt loop. I want to make sure that I don't lose a bracket overboard. I'm successful, until the last hole when the drill bit flies out of the chuck, bounces on deck, and splashes in the water.

Earlier, in a serious tone, Bill had explained, "Things happen and get broken. I'll not get upset about broken gear . . . if you are careful."

I finish the job and the hatch looks new.

* * * * * *

At mid-afternoon, Don comes by the boat to invite us to a party. Don is a Texan and his wife, Mimi, is a Californian turned Texan by their long marriage.

We arrive at Silver Cloud, a fifty-foot classic schooner, to find five SA guests already aboard. Joining everyone in the huge cockpit, we make our introductions and settle in for drinks and conversation.

(L to R) Earl, Don and Mimi aboard Silver Cloud

Bill has brought a naked can of something that looks like peanuts marked on the rusted metal. When he opens it, the huge #10 can of boiled peanuts becomes the topic of conversation. We answer questions about the eastern North Carolina delicacy and assure the group that boiled peanuts are not for everyday consumption, but a specialty for parties.

We tour the boat, examining several staterooms and the head forward, the well-equipped galley, the salon, and the large owner's stateroom and head aft. Everything is gleaming and perfect with a woman's decorative touch. Mimi calls us together for snacks around the large salon table.

* * * * * *

Earl and Judy, a Johannesburg couple, are sailing with Earl's son and wife aboard for a holiday junket. They recently rounded Cape Agulhas on the trip westward from near Johannesburg. Nathan, Earl's father, has met the boat here and will sail home singlehanded while the others make the return trip by land.

The conversation shifts to Don and Mimi's ten years of travel. Soft-spoken Don spins a few tales of travels in the Caribbean. Bill talks a bit about his circumnavigation.

Mimi finds an American road atlas so Bill and I can show the party where we live in eastern North Carolina. We answer questions about U.S. politics, economics, and geography; questions neither one of us is qualified to discuss, but we do so anyway.

Back aboard Advent II, we end the evening with the decision to attempt to go on anchor tomorrow night. A Monday morning departure will be nice, but we acknowledge, it really all depends on the wind!

Sunday, Jan 16, 2005

Lasting Impression from a Sunday Church Service

The St. Francis of Assisi Parish Anglican Church was founded in the late 1700s with the present building built in the early 1900s. We enter a crowded hall that has white stucco walls supporting large exposed timber rafters. The pews, very old and rustic, creak loudly under my bulk.

The service is tedious as I try to understand the heavily accented priest; however, I easily recognize the common cup communion. The most touching part of the service is when the congregation sings a special song with a dirge-like cadence.

God Bless Africa

If you believe and I take heed,
United against AIDS,
With love and care we'll conquer all,
South Africa will be saved.

If you believe and I take heed,
United against AIDS,
We'll fight our fear with truth and love,
South Africa will be saved.

Today believe, today take heed.
Unite with us we pray.
With hearts inspired we'll heed the call,
For God will lead the way.

Africa today is a miracle! Racial relations are very good with the new black government seemingly doing an outstanding job. The huge problem is HIV/AIDS. In 2005, newscasts put the number of HIV-positive people at five million (10% of the population), however, Bill has heard a healthcare worker claim the numbers are more like 27%. Over three hundred thousand people died of AIDS in 2004. This added thousands to the register of two million orphans who depend on society for care.

The older population is relatively untouched; however, the younger productive population is 80% HIV-positive. South African thinkers worry that within ten years the country could descend into anarchy as a result of the lawlessness from economic depravity caused by the inability to work, the cost of orphan care, and the enormous cost of caring for so many sick people.

At the same time, the country is experiencing a brain drain as educated citizens flee the country. Business owners are required to submit to a 51% black ownership, a requirement which leads to decisions to abandon assets and flee, or stay and cope.

Knowing the political and AIDS facts and hearing the congregation sing *God Bless Africa* in such a serious voice is one of the most touching moments of my life.

* * * * * *

After the service, several people in the congregation make a point to welcome us. We linger in conversation and then look at commemorative plaques on the walls that honor lost seaman. One church window shaped wooden plaque reads:

This tablet is erected by his shipmates in memory of Hugh St. Clair Hammill, Midshipman of H.M.S. Narrissus, who was killed by a fall from the Main-top, while exerrising (sic) off the Island of Ascension, March 7, 1863. Aged 19. - So he bringeth (sic) them unto the heaven where they would be.

We shake hands with the priest as we walk out into a bright windy day. Later, we find that the church lost 70% of their membership in 1976 when Simon's Town was declared "White Only" during the Apartheid era. This was a crushing blow to the church that sees no difference in the skin color of their members.

* * * * * *

It's Sunday afternoon and we are making last-minute departure preparations. Bill removes Windy from storage, mounts her on the stern, and rigs the steering lines as I try to absorb the logic and function. Bill tells me how to set a course while using Windy, but I will need several more demonstrations while underway to gain any proficiency.

The ship's water tanks are topped off again and the on-deck emergency water jugs are filled, chlorinated, and lashed in place. Folding metal deck chairs are stowed, a new mainsheet is rigged, the operation of the bilge pump is checked, and the emergency GPS is checked and hidden. Bill explains that hiding a GPS is prudent, as boarding pirates usually steal all electronics. It would be disastrous being caught at sea without a way to navigate.

Bill's current plan is to move the boat out to the anchorage then leave early Monday morning. We'll motor sail directly into the southeast wind to Cape Hangklip at the east side of False Bay, then tack ninety degrees to sail southwest, leaving Cape Point on our starboard by at least five to ten miles. This maneuver takes ten to twelve hours but will help us avoid the confused seas close to the Cape Point/Cape of Good Hope area. We need a calmer period of at least twelve hours to make our rounding and offing to cross the shipping lanes and find the calmer trade winds to Saint Helena Island.

* * * * * *

Late in the afternoon, Don from Silver Cloud stops me on the dock to engage in a serious conversation. We spent the prior lovely evening aboard his yacht with other cruising friends. I gave a present to the hostess—a small bag of hard candy of a kind favored by cruisers as a diversion on long watches.

"I want to return these, Jim," he said. "You see I'm seventy-one years old and have a special diet—lots of fruits, vegetables, no candy—as I try to beat this thing. I have CLL or CCC, or whatever they call this blood cancer."

I am taken aback that he has chosen to share with me.

"We're selling the boat. I think we may find a little place to live in Puerto Rico. My wife eats what I eat, so I thought you might like to have the candy back."

Not knowing what to say, I realize that he just needs someone to talk to. We spend a while just talking about nothing, as sailors do before Don ambles off to his boat.

Another fact sifts through my muddled brain. Although I have yet to sail offshore on a single extended ocean voyage, I have already, by association, been accepted into the cruising fraternity. He has accepted my friendship and confidence.

I have become a Cruising Yachtie.

While standing on the dock with Don, the wind whips at our clothes and howls in nearby riggings. It's blowing too hard to move the boat. We'll spend another night with all the comforts of shore life. Maybe tomorrow the wind will slow enough for us to get underway.

Monday, Jan 17, 2005

The morning is bright and clear, but the persistent thirty- to forty-knot wind is just too much for our sailing escape. Bill gets current weather information on the SSB, a forecast calling for strong winds that may last until Friday. It's not supposed to blow this hard at this time of the year!

Yesterday, Bill tried to install one of the new oil filters to verify all is right. Not so! The new oil filter has a central pipe diameter that is a tad smaller than required. Another trip to Midas is required to fetch the correct oil filter.

Instrument showing 45 Knots while docked at FBYC.

We find two filters that have a little smaller capacity than the original but will fit our needs. This is a compromise, but at last, we have usable filters.

At the Pick-N-Pay we buy more melons, some sweets, and minor stuff, and flag a Rikkis for the trip home. Bill and I are sitting on the back seat when the driver picks up a new rider for the front seat, then stops for four adults and a small boy. That makes nine bodies in the minibus taxi—a record from my observations.

* * * * * *

On our return, we find the wind still blowing—45 knots as I write.

We've again abandoned plans to go on anchor. The wind is just too high for such a maneuver. Maybe we will have a favorable break in the weather tomorrow!

Tuesday, Jan 18, 2005

Attempting Our Sailing Departure

✦ ✦ ✦

Bill's Email Dispatch

Underway from Simon's Town at 0700 hours. The plan is to go directly into the wind, across False Bay, then when we reach the other side about 1100 hours, turn southwest putting the wind on the port beam and Cape of Good Hope about ten miles off to starboard. We will sail about ten miles into the Atlantic before turning northwest.

✦ ✦ ✦

Bill is awake often during the night in anticipation of departure. I get up at 0400 hours to help him worry. The weather report is favorable so the Captain abandons plans to go to anchor and decides to immediately get underway.

We leave the docks in bright sunny weather with a clear sky and winds less than ten knots. Rounding the point of the naval shipyard breakwater, we encounter large waves and rising wind.

About noon, after motoring into rising winds and rather large seas, we make the southwest turn and begin a broad reach into the large waves. Bill has sent an email announcing our departure and then listens to Alistair, a weather guru who interprets the weather for large sections of ocean, give the weather report announcing a gale warning for Cape Point.

I had been steering the whole morning, enjoying the feel of a real boat smashing into large waves.

Bill comes topside and says, "Let's Come About!"

I bring the boat about and immediately the ride becomes more tolerable. I even add a scrap more of the furling genny as we motor sail back to the False Bay Yacht Club and the safety of our old slip.

A sailor on the dock welcomes us home by commenting with that tired phrase, "They don't call it the Cape of Storms for nothing."

Chapter 2

First Leg: Sailing to Saint Helena Island

 Day #1, Wednesday, Jan 19, 2005

✦   ✦   ✦

<u>*Bill's Email Dispatch*</u>

This morning we waited until Alistair was on the radio. He said that strong (20-30 knots) winds are forecast for Cape Point today, no gales. He said that it is probably a good time for us to leave.

We were underway in 15 minutes, leaving Simon's Town at 0915 hours. Once again the plan is to motor into the 17-knot wind until we get near to the other side, then put the wind on the port side to clear the cape. At 3.5 knots, it may take awhile.

✦   ✦   ✦

At dawn, there is a heavy overcast sky with little wind. On the SSB, Alistair makes it clear that Cape Point weather is "about as good as it gets!" and will remain so for the next day or two, then turn bad into next week.

Bill issues a terse, "Let's go!"

We cast off lines and I man the helm as Bill deflates dock fenders and putters about on deck. At the breakwater and Simon's Town lighthouse, we encounter ten- to fifteen-knot winds but the swell is not as bad as yesterday. Cape Hangklip is just visible on the horizon cloud cover.

As Cape Point comes into view to starboard, the upper half is covered in clouds—the way a mysterious cape should look. After a short sail toward Cape Hangklip, Bill changes the plan of the day and abruptly orders an one hundred eighty degree (south) course that will take us directly to the east of Cape Point. By omitting the long sail across the bay and tack to gain a position south of Cape Point, we're taking a chance that the conditions will be calm enough at the cape to allow our escape.

🦋 🦋 🦋

Bill's Email Dispatch

Rounded Cape Point at 13:30 and at 14:00 we are headed west to make sea room. All is well.

🦋 🦋 🦋

With increasing waves and wind, we arrive off a docile Cape Point and are able to round it with relative ease. The southeast wind holds as we motor sail into the dense fog over the Benguela Current. Bill keeps a close radar watch for the big tankers and freighters that round this point close in to avoid as much current as possible. At nightfall, after dinner, Bill has the first watch. I retire.

At midnight, I wake to eight clear strikes of the ship's bell. I put on my foul weather jacket and inflatable life vest, hang the mini flashlight lanyard around my neck and buckle on my safety harness. This ensemble, with or without the foul weather jacket, will rule my life for the next two months.

The watch is set in the navy tradition of sounding eight bells on the brass ship's bell. I get used to my wake-up order: Ding-ding, ding-ding, ding-ding, ding-ding! It is about as good a method to rouse out of sleep as any other.

Rounding a foggy Cape Point.

The kitchen timer begins another rule of my life. The timer is set to ten minutes. When it rings, the watch crewman resets it for ten more minutes and goes topside to look for ship traffic, and to check the sail set, the boat speed, and track required by the GPS. The ten-minute timer rule will operate twenty four hours a day for the entire trip. We are less formal during daylight, but one crewman is still responsible for the helm and answers the annoying timer.

* * * * * *

My first thunderstorm at sea is imminent. Bill stays with me as we watch the approaching storm on radar, and then experience its awesome power and terror. Lightning illuminates visible foaming crests on the black sea to reveal the enormous size of the swell. The interval between lightning flashes and the crash of thunder shortens as the storm approaches. For a brief period, the flash and sound seem instantaneous, then the interval lengthens to indicate the passing of the intruder.

With the storm past, Bill retires while I sit in the cockpit trying to stay warm and alert. I marvel at Windy as she steers the boat with authority. Even in huge following waves that appear about to swamp us, this trusty wind vane steers us clear and back on course without fail.

Bill says the wind vane is the single most important item that makes a cruising sailing life possible. This device steers all the time, freeing a crewman of the chore. Manually steering the boat 24 hours a day would be a huge task.

Alone in the cockpit, the helm moves by itself as Windy keeps our boat on course. I will watch her steer unassisted the entire 5,400 miles to Trinidad.

Lighted dials on the GPS and the VHF radio glow and keep me company. The night is dark with only subtle changes in black marking the horizon. Breaking waves have a faint glow of phosphoresce that makes them stand out stark white against the black sea.

Otherwise, everything is black—the sky, the sea, my mood!

The radar display, our electronic lookout for ships, is out of the weather inside the main companionway. I sit, cold and unneeded, staring at the display and keeping a lookout for trouble.

At 0330 hours, "Beep, Beep, Beep!" is the radar warning. I spot the lights of a ship off our starboard stern, strike a sharp warning on the ship's bell, and yell, "Captain on deck!"

Normally, you would simply watch the approaching vessel and take action if a collision seems possible. However, I am new and under night orders to call the Captain if I encounter any ship traffic. Bill takes the watch early and the ship passes safely by our stern.

Filled with the excitement of rounding one of the world's most dangerous points of land, surviving my first thunderstorm at sea, and encountering a ship on a black night at sea, I plop into my warm bunk and fade into well-deserved sleep.

James E. Keen

Day #2, Thursday, Jan 20, 2005
Noon Position: 33 deg. 43 min S, 16 deg. 3 min E
1,585 nautical miles to Saint Helena
Noon-to-Noon Run: 165 nautical miles

❧ ❧ ❧

<u>Bill's Email Dispatch</u>

I set the reefed trysail and small staysail, anticipating stronger wind, and we motor sailed at 180° past the Cape of Storms. The clouds continued to settle and now we are fogged in. I have the anchor light and radar on and feel relatively secure. As we went by, the radar showed Cape Point so I verified it is working. I will leave it on as long as we have this fog. It is cold.

Jim steered all the way until we shut off the engine and Windy took over. We took a lot of water on deck motoring against the wind and waves, and part of the time I was on deck raising the sails, so I am damp and salty. I think it will be an evening for a sponge bath. About 1330 hours I cooked a pot of rice with some onions, and about 1430 hours, when we went on the vane, Jim opened a can of stuff and some peaches, and we had a good meal for a cold day.

It is 1600 hours now and we are 15 nautical miles southwest of Cape Point, sailing less than 5 knots. I am very conservative; I don't trust this weather. I plan to stay on this 260° course for a few more hours, then probably go wing-n-wing a little north of west. I want about 100 miles of sea room before I go on a northwest course to Saint Helena.

(Bill writes about his adventures only while at sea. This piece was sent as part of the morning broadcast email.)

74

Trinidad Express

South Africa:

I do not know when the western world first became aware of The East but surely Rome knew of the lands across the deserts. Marco Polo first visited the area in 1271, and thereafter people sought a practical trading route. Ships, sent by Prince Henry the Navigator of Portugal, searched the west coast of Africa, farther and farther until, in 1488, four years before Columbus came to the new world, Portuguese ships rounded the south end of the continent and started across the Indian Ocean. Undoubtedly Columbus knew of the discovery, but at the time cartography was a most guarded national secret. Without charts, trying to follow the Portuguese was like, in the 1960s, another country following the U.S. to the moon. The route around Africa soon became well known, however.

The Dutch were major world merchants and set up the Dutch East India Company in 1602, 110 years after Columbus and 5 years before Jamestown. The Dutch East India Company controlled all commerce with the east and had military as well as civil authority in the area. Controlling the southern tip of Africa was critical to commerce, and an outpost was settled at Cape Town for the summer months and Simon's Town for the winter months. The prevailing winds reverse summer and winter.

These settlements were primarily concerned with commerce around the cape, but support functions were needed, and soon farming and industry started, with a corresponding increase in the Dutch population.

About 200 years later the British were expanding their world influence and realized that controlling the route around Africa was critical to protecting their military as well as commercial interest. The Dutch were allied with the French at the time, and London was afraid that the French would occupy and control the area. The British took Cape Town in 1795. (Read The Mauritius Command by Patrick O'Brian for more on British influence in the area.) All that the British were interested in was protecting the sea route and no effort was made at colonizing the area. The sizable Dutch population migrated inland to escape English domination.

The native kingdoms in southern Africa were becoming organized, which reached a climax with the Zulu ruler King Shaka, who starting in 1817, waged war on and devastated other lands in the area. The people of what is now central South Africa migrated north as refugees, and when King Shaka withdrew to the Zulu homeland in northeastern South Africa, central SA was largely uninhabited.

The Dutch prospered as farmers and the population increased. The Dutch migration goal was to establish a nation between the Vaal and Limpopo Rivers. This is across the Vaal and this area, the bushveldt, became known as Transvaal, and the people called Afrikaner. Johannesburg and Pretoria are located here.

The population increase and the expansion of farming inevitably led to conflicts with the Zulu. At the Battle of Blood River (Buffalo River, which flows to the sea at East London) where the river ran red with blood, the Afrikaners established boundaries between them and the Zulu.

The British, still concerned with maritime and military passage around the cape, did not encroach on the Afrikaner territory until gold and diamonds were discovered in the 1860s. The Afrikaners, being largely agricultural, were slow to exploit these new riches, and the British moved in. Their first major conflict was with the Zulu. When it came to gold and diamonds the British did not respect the Transvaal / Zulu frontier. The Zulu resisted, culminating in the Zulu War in 1879. (Zulu, a motion picture available on video, is an account of this war.)

The British eventually subdued the Zulu, but their increasing control over all aspects of life in the area increasingly antagonized the Afrikaners, who rebelled in 1899 to overthrow the British and establish a free nation. The Boer War lasted three years and was a black mark in British history. The British vastly outnumbered the Afrikaners, who had met their match, until the British started a scorched earth policy that devastated the land and forced everyone (Afrikaners) into concentration camps. Over 25,000 Afrikaner women and children died at the hands of the British. That was only 100 years ago.

Hard feelings remain. The British won the war, but could not govern the country, and after much negotiation created the Union of South Africa in 1910 and withdrew. The Union of South Africa was a self-governing protectorate. The document giving self-government contained the clause, ". . . (delay) the question of granting a franchise to natives until after self-government has been established."

Meanwhile, the indigenous population was migrating back into South Africa. The native population grew, threatening the Afrikaners. The government understood that the natives needed a place to call their own, and established Territorial separation of black and white ownership of land. This was the beginning of Apartheid.

The harder the blacks pushed for equality, the harder the government repressed them. The seeds of the crisis were sown in 1964 when exclusion zones were established. For example, Simon's Town was a white zone. All blacks were forcefully removed. In the museum, there is a picture of the Anglican Church with a caption that it lost 70% of its communicants when the blacks and coloureds were removed. Business leaders, the churches, and civic organizations formally objected, but the government carried out the order.

South Africa became an international pariah. With the situation growing steadily worse, it was a tinderbox ready to ignite and destroy the country.

We were talking to a white taxi driver in Cape Town whose brother is in politics. The driver told us a story that his brother had told him 30 years earlier. A young lawyer, F.W. de Klerk, was entering politics and the political experts were telling him that this young lawyer would someday be Prime Minister, and would end Apartheid. When de Klerk came into office he allowed people like Desmond Tutu and Peter Storey to negotiate the release of Nelson Mandela, who had been in prison for 24 years. Mandela was released, and the new South Africa emerged. It took about four years of a transitional government to create a new

77

constitution, and then in 1994 the first free, universal election was held. There was equality for all. Apparently, they mean it.

⚡ ⚡ ⚡

Today the sea is moderate, although still huge for my Pamlico Sound experience. Fog and the thunderstorm from last night are forgotten and the weather begins to clear.

Shipboard life is one of constant motion. I soon learn the pattern of the boat's motion; however, any odd motion sends me flying out of control. Items not properly stowed end up on the sole.

In the sharp motion of the boat, my life depends on: the four-point hold (hold on with two feet and two hands); three-point hold (two feet and one hand); and two-point hold (two feet). The boat's motions include: a lurch when riding up waves, an equally sharp pitch when riding down into a rut in the ocean, and a rolling heel which is a violent swing as much as forty-five degrees from side to side. When running directly ahead of the wind, without the steadying effect of a side wind on the sails, she will heel in a period that could take several seconds or be as fast as two seconds, sometimes burying the lee gunwale in the green water. Once she starts a roll, it often goes on and on for an extended period before dampening out.

* * * * * *

We fall into a familiar shipboard routine.

Typical day: 0000 hours to 0400 hours is my watch and then Bill takes the 0400 hours to 0800 hours watch. I try to take over Bill's watch early, about 0700 hours, to give him time to use the SSB, have his personal clean-up time, and then a two-hour nap. As Bill sleeps, I catch up on my computer log and correspondence, have personal clean-up time, and use the cockpit bucket.

78

Mornings and afternoons are free time with someone volunteering to answer the nagging ten-minute timer. However, both of us are watchful and generally aware of conditions.

Late afternoon is shower time. We take turns at a sponge bath in the cockpit followed by a shower of clean, hot, fresh water from the garden pressure sprayer. Each of us has to heat a kettle of water on the galley stove to add to the tepid water in the pressure sprayer. It's worth the effort to feel clean for the evening meal.

Bill takes an hour long nap at 1900 hours before starting his 2000 hours watch. I sleep until my 0000 hours watch and the start of a new day.

Bill working at the mast as we fly a reefed Trysail and partially furled Genoa.

Our meals are inelegant, but not Spartan. Morning meals consist of fruit snacks in anticipation of the one-pot main meal of the day. Bill eats oatmeal some mornings that he soaks in tepid UHT boxed milk. For lunch, I put two cups of rice in the pressure cooker, along with any vegetable I think might be good. Onions keep well on the boat and we use lots of them. When the rice is cooked, I open the pressure cooker and put in a can of meat or fish. I close the cooker and when we are hungry, we eat our fill. We add another can of meat to the leftovers and eat it for dinner together as a more formal meal.

Artisan bread, with no preservatives, goes bad quickly, so we keep it in an airy hammock net near the galley along with oranges, carrots, and pineapple, the fresh items we intend to eat first.

We drink a minimum of four liters of water each day. Dehydration can sneak up on you with the strong sunlight and the drying effects of wind. I carry my two-liter water bottle about, sipping frequently, a habit I continue in my shore life today.

The Captain's standing sailing order is to log the GPS position at the beginning of each watch. Bill takes the noon position and plots it on a small scale chart that shows the entire South Atlantic, the whole area between South America and Africa. The daily distance run plot shows varied-length lines ending with a circle around a dot as the plotted position fix. This awkward line is rarely straight but the general line is towards the destination. I had hoped Bill would give me this plot as a souvenir at the end of the trip. He did. It's now proudly displayed on my office wall.

Formal watches and sleep punctuate our life filled with glorious sailing days and some miserable days on a lonely lovely sea.

Day #3, Friday, Jan 21, 2005
Noon Position: 32 deg. 65 min S, 13 deg. 37 min E
1,429 nautical miles to Saint Helena
Noon-to-Noon Run: 156 nautical miles

🪶   🪶   🪶

Bill's Email Dispatch

This is probably the finest sailing I have ever done. The sea is comfortable; wind about 15 knots on the starboard quarter, boat speed in the mid-5s. But the thing that makes it so much fun is the 1- to 2-knot positive current helping us along. Speed over ground is in the mid-7s.

We traveled 165 nautical miles yesterday. That equals the best I have ever done.

🪶   🪶   🪶

Today is bright and sunny with only puffy white clouds in the sky. This is like trade wind sailing, but we're not supposed to get to the trade wind belt for several hundred more miles. Alistair says that we'll likely have this weather all the way to Saint Helena.

Windy steering on a calm day.

81

Day #4, Saturday, Jan 22, 2005
Noon Position: 30 deg. 40 min S, 11 deg. 31 min E
1,291 nautical miles to Saint Helena
Noon-to-Noon Run: 138 nautical miles

🐾 🐾 🐾

Bill's Email Dispatch

Sometime overnight we lost the wonderful 1- to 2-knot positive current, but the perfect sailing conditions continue. The wind is about 12 knots on the port beam and the boat is going about 6.5 knots. The amazing thing is that the seas are very comfortable. The boat is heeled a little, and absolutely stable. I can walk in the cabin without holding on (two point hold). This is luxury.

The wind speed indicator stopped working. The cups do not spin and just sit there. I guess the gales at Simon's Town were too much for it. I will miss it. I enjoy it, and it is important to know what is going on. For example, right now Jim is topside. I would like to be able to glance up and see the wind speed on the display at the navigation desk.

🐾 🐾 🐾

Fresh fruit is a favorite onboard. We still have six honeydew melons, a big sack of oranges, several whole pineapples, a few green peppers, onions, and raw carrots.

Bill made a special treat for lunch today. We have lots of canned mackerel aboard, but there's one problem—it stinks! Your hands smell like strong fish as soon as you touch the stuff. However, Bill and I like it. He removes and discards the bone from the canned fish, mashes up the flesh, then adds crackers and an egg to make fish patties. The fried cakes are wonderful and the fishy smell is gone. The leftover single-pot dish is rice with black beans and onions. It is a great meal!

Trinidad Express

Day #5, Sunday, Jan 23, 2005
Noon Position: 29 deg. 24 min S, 10 deg. 7 min E
1,187 nautical miles to Saint Helena
Noon-to-Noon Run: 104 nautical miles

❧ ❧ ❧

<u>Bill's Email Dispatch</u>

Last night was totally overcast with light wind. Sailing was slow as we have lost the very helpful current. Today is absolutely beautiful, with a deep blue sky, calm seas, and not much wind. We will run the engine when the wind dies, then go back to sailing when it picks up. It is one of those idyllic days, very relaxing. Read, or snooze, or peck away at the computer.

❧ ❧ ❧

My day is filled with reading in the cockpit. It's uncomfortable to read with sunglasses; but they are necessary in the bright glare of reflections, especially with the artificial lens in my left eye from cataract surgery. I read the first book of the <u>Left Behind</u> series while in California in December, so I'm reading four more of the series that I brought along. They are somewhat tedious, but my daughter Dianne wants me to read them.

Bill cleans drawers. He has a really big drawer at the navigation station, a catchall. It's more like a plastic tub, with lots of stuff thrown inside. He spends the afternoon sorting and actually throws out a lot.

Bill and Normandie had developed a conscious plan for being frugal and ecologically sound aboard Advent II. We monitor our water usage. Bill shows me how to wash dishes in one pan of soapy water, and then rinse each dish by using a pistol spray bottle filled with fresh water.

We find a second use for things aboard, but food scraps, cans, and paper cartons are thrown overboard. Plastic and other unusable trash are bagged for disposal on land. The one-pot meals save on prep time, propane, cleanup, and with the pressure cooker secured with the stove fiddles, it is the only way that you can cook in rough seas. Each person uses one plate and fork (or spoon) and eats while sitting down in a braced position.

Bill's advice is, "Put it on the sole first. It'll end up there anyway!"

Sailing Wing-to-Wing on a calm sea.

Day #6, Monday, Jan 24, 2005
Noon Position: 28 deg. 17 min S, 8 deg. 32 min E
1,080 nautical miles to Saint Helena
Noon-to-Noon Run: 107 nautical miles

☙ ☙ ☙

Bill's Email Dispatch

No wind, motoring since 0700 hours. Alistair said that this calm may continue through Wednesday. Maybe there is enough wind to ripple the surface and we can sail between 2 and 3 knots. The sea is calm with just a gentle swaying as we move through the water. It is a very lazy time.

Now, let's go back to our arrival in South Africa (SA). At Richards Bay, the first thing I noticed was the buoys. They were all there, in place and new looking. The buoyage is better than I am used to in the U.S. and there are operating lighthouses within sight of each other all along the SA coast. Richards Bay is a modern deep water port and the marina where we stayed is a modern full-service marina. It is located among upscale shops and restaurants that typically develop at modern waterfronts. The town of Richards Bay was created about 30 years ago when the harbor was developed, and nothing is more than 30 years old.

It is laid out like a very large planned community with large open spaces for future development. In the central business district, there are modern stores and a lot of parking. The residential areas have nice houses, and the streets are wide and in good repair. Many people say it looks like the new areas of the U.S. southwest. Everywhere we went in Richards Bay or the Cape Town area, the roads were similar to the U.S. and almost everywhere we went had four-lane roads. The drivers are better than the U.S. with most people obeying the rules. There is an easy flow of traffic.

But, you know you are not in the U.S. when you see the hippopotamus crossing signs; a sign, like a deer warning sign, but with a picture of a hippo. We went on a game safari. At 0500 hours a gaggle

85

of yachties piled into a small van. We were the only native English speakers in the bunch. We headed north into King Shaka's land. A large part of the Shaka Zulu land is now a national game park—hundreds of square miles. We were in the northeast part of SA, Zulu country. For this one day safari, we drove the roads of part of the park, the driver getting information on where game had been spotted. The guide searched for a herd of elephants, but when on safari, some days you are successful and some days you are not. It was a very good glimpse of the way Africa used to be, although, in this part of the country, people still have to be careful at night because of lions.

On the ride up and back we went through several land uses. Most noticeable were the tree farms, just like eastern North Carolina, except growing eucalyptus—called gum trees here, and in Australia its Kookaburra (. . . sits in the old gum tree . . .). There were also pineapple and sugar cane fields. Most of the houses along the way were just plain small rural houses, but about 15% were round, with thatched roofs. The old way of living was in round huts, and the old folks are more comfortable living in their round cottages beside their children in their square houses.

Noticeable are mass produced porta-potty outhouses. It was obvious that the government was taking action to better public health. We never had to question the drinking water. It was good wherever we went.

❦ ❦ ❦

It was good sailing weather last night and we now have morning calm. Bill starts the diesel and we motor from 0715 hours to 1500 hours. The wind does return for an afternoon broad reach with main and jib flying. The wind holds nicely overnight.

Bill digs in a locker for Normandie's fishing gear and asks me to try my luck. Neither of us is a fisherman; however, I have used a hand line a few times. I set two hand lines behind the boat for three to four hours with not one sign of a fish being attracted to the Clark Spoon that I offer.

We see flying fish most days, leaping into the air all at once like a covey of quail. They fly low over the waves, skipping a time or two like a stone skipped across a pond. Many mornings, we clean stiff dried flying fish from the deck. I wish they were good to eat.

Maybe my fishing luck will be better another day.

Day #7, Tuesday, Jan 25, 2005
Noon Position: 27 deg. 7 min S, 6 deg. 47 min E
963 nautical miles to Saint Helena
Noon-to-Noon Run: 117 nautical miles

Frequent squalls punctuate this overcast and rainy day. On my midnight watch, I was able to cross the main to the port side so that we're now flying wing-n-wing. Our big genoa jib is held on a pole to starboard while the mainsail is boomed to port with a preventer rig set to avoid an accidental gibe. The wind comes from straight behind the boat now, an attitude we hope will continue all the way home.

This type of sailing gives rise to the famous cruiser's saying, "Gentlemen never sail to windward!" Cruising sailors have time on their side, so they select routes and departure times that will give them wind from astern.

With rain squalls in the area, we have been hesitant to fly the mainsail. Instead, we switch to the trysail, our normal heavier and smaller nighttime sail. You never know how much wind is in a squall, so you want to be able to lower sails in a hurry. The mainsail takes forever to secure, with one of us climbing on the coachroof to corral and tie the sail to the boom. We are cautious in its use and fly it only in settled weather. The trysail is stronger and smaller, so we can fly it in most any weather, including squalls. We do fly the big genoa most of the time because it can be quickly and easily furled from the cockpit by using the headstay roller furling rig.

I've been planning all morning for our meeting with Valdivia Bank where the ocean bottom rises to only 69 feet deep. I expect crazy currents, maybe large swells or breaking seas, and maybe fishing boats on the shoals. We're trying to time our arrival for daylight hours so we avoid the possible danger at night. Maybe I'll try a fishing line when we arrive.

Day #8, Wednesday, Jan 26, 2005
Noon Position: 26 deg. 15 min S, 5 deg. 7 min E
853 nautical miles to Saint Helena
Noon-to-Noon Run: 110 nautical miles

<hr />

Bill's Email Dispatch

We have only seen a few birds since we left, and no other life. We have been alone out here. Then yesterday we ran through many schools (squadrons?) of flying fish. Last night I was standing in the cockpit when I felt something bump my hip, then fall to my foot. Wondering what had fallen, I turned on the AA cell flashlight that hangs around my neck at night. Flopping on the floor was a frustrated flying fish. We often find them on deck, but this was the first time one has come in the cockpit with me. We also find squid on deck, and sometimes they are quite large, maybe 10" long.

The fish Coelacanth (latimeria chalumnae) appeared about 350 million years ago and were abundant throughout much of the world. The genus coelanthus has been found as fossils in rocks from the end of the Permian (245 million years ago) to the end of the Jurassic (144 million years ago). Coelacanth had heavy bodies with four highly mobile limb-like fins and are thought to be the predecessors of all land creatures. It was believed to be extinct, but in 1938 Marjorie Latimer identified a specimen taken off the coast of Africa. Rewards were offered, but it was not until 1952 that a second was obtained. Since then several others have been caught in the area.

On to East London:

We made a one day hop to Durban, a modern, industrialized city with an impressive skyline of high-rise buildings. The Wild Coast south of Durban was the longest stretch without safe harbor. We had to time

89

it right or we would get it wrong. The wind was right, the forecast right and we escaped from Durban, and comfortably made the sail. East London, on the Buffalo River, is the only river port in South Africa.

The Ncome River is the infamous Blood River, where the Voortrekkers (Dutch and Afrikaans pioneer farmers) massacred Zulu until the river ran red with blood. This is still Zulu and Afrikaans country. A very beautiful river flows between mountains that look like a movie scene. Day tour boats take tourists up the river, a trip that we would have liked to have taken except that we were still playing the weather windows.

Entering the port, the first thing you notice is the cars lined up on the commercial dock. Every few days a ship comes and takes away the product of a Daimler-Chrysler assembly plant nearby. A short distance upstream is a bridge over the river with yachts moored on the left and Latimer's Landing on the right. This is the place that the recent tsunami flooded the harbor, and a dozen boats were adrift in East London. The NSRI (National Sea Rescue Institute) tugs and utility vessels managed to contain major damage which was flooding out to sea or breaking masts under de bridge over de Buffalo River.

Latimer's Landing is a tourist type place with restaurants, shops, and slips for visiting yachts. On the boardwalk in a monument with the inscription, "Latimer's Landing—Proudly named after Marjorie Courtenay-Latimer—Who saved for science the Coelacanth". This is where it happened—at the little fishing village of East London.

I worry about closing on the Valdivia Seamount and shoals during my midnight watch but go off watch without noticing any signs of the shallows. When I came on watch at 0730 hours, Bill calmly says, "It's over there several miles!" All I see is water; no breaking waves, no mysterious currents, no fishing boats, and no dragons!

The seamount is approximately the midpoint of our journey to Saint Helena Island. We're both looking forward to real showers, fresh greens, and beer.

Early this morning, Bill set the drifter for the first time since I've been aboard. It's a very large, but lightweight, sail designed for providing a powerful boost in light winds. The drifter is not mounted on the roller furling gear but hanked on the forestay. It has to be manually lowered, gathered, and tied to the lifeline. With the huge drifter poled out on the port side and the big genoa poled out on the starboard side, we are truly wing-n-wing in the cruiser's sense. The drifter pulls hard like a mule, which is how it gets its nickname, Mule.

Day #9, Thursday, Jan 27, 2005
Noon Position: 24 deg. 52 min S, 3 deg. 52 min E
756 nautical miles to Saint Helena
Noon-to-Noon Run: 97 nautical miles

☘ ☘ ☘

Bill's Email Dispatch

We only made 97 miles yesterday. It was good sailing during the day, but the wind died during the night. The sea is so calm the sails do not flog when the wind drops, so there is no automatic trip to tell us that it is time to furl the genoa and start motoring.

We need to keep moving because we were six days late leaving Simon's Town and we need to make up that time. We made up one day the first day out, but have stayed the same since. Grayson's wedding is Easter weekend. Get me to the church in time. Hopefully, we will find a little more wind in the days to come. Until then we will motor when the wind drops.

South Africa, parting impressions:

South Africa is a modern country. The infrastructure works. Electricity, telephone, highways, water, sewage, medical care, fire departments and EMS, all are up to U.S. standards and in some cases surpass U.S. standards. It is obvious they have looked at other countries and adopted the systems they feel fits their country. Traffic is orderly and all the streets we saw were free of trash.

Of course, the streets are clean because people are paid $10 a day to keep them clean, but the people who clean the streets, or direct traffic in a parking lot, or clean the beaches, seem to have some pride in what they are doing.

The people, black and white, were the friendliest we have met anywhere. I cannot stress that enough. Strangers and acquaintances alike went out of their way to be friendly and helpful. Amazingly, and we were at some party type places, there was no loud music in SA! In the bars, yes. But we never heard the loud, and we find very obnoxious, music that the rest of the world thinks is necessary for people to have a good time.

Just 11 years ago, a black person could not vote. Now they are a thriving democracy. Housing is distinct by racial and religious lines, with black, white, Moslem and Hindu areas, but in public, all people are accepted and found everywhere. I do not know if any blacks are yacht club members, but I have seen blacks swimming on the club beach, so I guess so.

SA has gotten so prosperous that a large percentage of the population is overweight, and lifestyle diabetes is getting to be a problem. In the past ten years, SA has become a major world player. It is the unquestioned leader in Africa, negotiating between conflicting groups in other parts of the continent. SA troops are part of peacekeeping forces around the world. I heard a BBC program asking if the Euro would replace the dollar as the world currency. One expert said that in the future the world currency would be a combination of the dollar, Euro, something that China would develop, and the South African Rand. And, I am glad to say, the politics seem to be healthy. People that I talked to, black and white, give Nelson Mandela the credit. A test will come when he passes.

I was very impressed with South Africa.

But there are huge problems that must be overcome. Unemployment is 40%, and the social programs cannot deal with the poverty in parts of the country. But still, SA is the land of opportunity to people from other African countries. Along the highways groups of people from Zimbabwe, or Namibia, Botswana, or Ivory Coast, illegal immigrants, are trying to sell jewelry or carvings to make enough money to live. The immigration offices have large groups of people trying to get legal status. In addition to their own poverty, SA is dealing with an uncontrolled flow of aliens.

Now the dark side: crime is uncontrolled. The modern, comfortable train to Cape Town had two security guards on each coach and several at each station. Every shop will have a security guard. Not so much at the Cape, but in Richards Bay, Durban, and East London the houses are surrounded by high walls with concertina wire at the top and have burglar bars, security doors, and alarm systems. There are places one doesn't let anyone within a double arm's reach. One never walks, but always takes a taxi. (The exceptions are Simon's Town and Cape Town where I always felt absolutely comfortable.) The crime is due in part to the transition from tribal to modern cultures, and the oppression of the people in the past. Those that have not feel justified in taking from the rich. There are apparently three categories of criminals in SA.

Common criminals and organized crime are two with which every country struggles. The third is a larger threat than all of South Africa's other problems combined. In a country of 40 million people, 5 million have AIDS and some say 27% are HIV-positive. About 300,000 people died last year from AIDS.

A hungry person dying from AIDS thinks nothing of taking from the rich. There is a dread in South Africa that this is only the beginning. Our friend the dentist has a sister who is a physician in a rural area. She took part in a study of HIV and pregnancy. In her area, they could not find a pregnant woman who was not HIV-positive. Millions of children are growing up without parents or the extended family of the past. Those children are HIV-positive and having uncared for children of their own. These millions will multiply, with associated uncontrollable crime until the society itself will collapse. South Africa will descend into anarchy.

Every middle-class person in South Africa, black and white, has to make the decision whether to stay or leave for another country. Our friend, the dentist, who has made the decision to stay, said he can install security system on top of security system, but in the end, it will not stop the desperate and dying millions.

When we arrived in Simon's Town, Louie, a False Bay Yacht Club member, and fellow yachtie heard our VHF calls, answered us, helped us land and made us feel welcome. Our last night there he stopped me and asked about our South Africa experience. That led to a conversation about the sights we had seen and places visited. I told him that people in the U.S. have heard terms like Zulu, Transvaal, Boer and Afrikaans, (etc) but don't know what they mean in history, and I was trying to explain some of it.

He said all that was not important. The important thing is Apartheid and the years since. I said that we know about Apartheid because of the press, and I was just beginning to get a feeling for the South Africa now. Louie then went on to tell me that everything has changed. There really has been a miracle in the way people think about each other. Blacks and whites really are working together. The fear, the hatred, the resentment of the blacks against the whites for past wrongs, and resentment of whites against blacks for lost privilege, is not there. The country is strong, the country is united.

Bill: But what about AIDS? Alone, South Africa cannot overcome AIDS.

Louie: We will.

Bill: You can't. You don't have the resources.

Louie: We will. I will be taxed; the black man with money will be taxed. We will, together, as a country, do what it takes. We are now doing this together, and nothing can stop us.

Bill: There will be millions of children, millions of homeless children.

Louie: We will take them into our homes. We will build group homes. These are children of South Africa, and we will not let them starve. They are our children.

Bill: There is not enough money in all of South Africa to do that. The only way is to get help from the U.S. and the European Union.

Louie: If we cannot do it ourselves, we will go to the U.S. we will go to the EU, with our hat in our hand, but we will not let these children starve.

God bless South Africa!

Shirley, the folding dinghy is lashed behind Bill who is making bread in the cockpit.

Trinidad Express

Our day starts calm and overcast, so we run the engine for five hours. It's the start of what is to become a long series of days of motoring much of the time, in order to make headway and keep close to the time schedule. Bill is really afraid of standing up his daughter at the altar, so we are on a Trinidad Express.

The afternoon brings wind and glorious sailing. Bill makes bread, two loaves, which really turn out nicely. We decide he might try adding other things, like fruit, to the next loaf.

It takes a lot of work to make bread.

James E. Keen

Day #10, Friday, Jan 28, 2005
Noon Position: 23 deg. 33 min S, 2 deg. 20 min E
642 nautical miles to Saint Helena
Noon-to-Noon Run: 114 nautical miles

⚡ ⚡ ⚡

<u>Bill's Email Dispatch</u>

Very gradually the temperature is warming. At Simon's Town, we were sleeping under light blankets. I noticed the blankets when I went to bed last night and realized they were no longer being used. The first few nights out, my night watch uniform was a short-sleeved shirt, a heavy fleece pullover, a long-sleeved shirt, and a raincoat. After two days the raincoat stayed hanging on its hook. Then last night, I left off the fleece pullover.

We crossed the Tropic of Capricorn today, Lat 23°-26' S, and are officially back in the tropics. Today the sky is blue, the sea calm, wind less than 10 knots, and we have a case of the tropics, the first reported on board for many months. Jim is in the forward cabin reading and it is all I can do to lift my fingers to the keyboard. I just want to snooze. Things just don't seem all that important.

⚡ ⚡ ⚡

The motor drones on and on during the night watches. However, our day dawns with partial overcast skies and rising winds. We stop the noisy diesel as puffy clouds accompany 10 to 15 knots of wind. Our headsails are flown wing-n-wing all day in the manner that is becoming our working model.

With the wind more from the south and southwest, it has been somewhat chilly, especially at night. However, the days are steadily becoming warmer with a typical day now in the 70- to 75-degree range. The bright, but the cloudless sky is flawless. When the wind blows

98

without clouds, there is little evidence of wind except for catspaws that flash over the ocean swell. When the wind stills, the boat sits with the sails slating back and forth, going nowhere.

That quickly becomes tiresome!

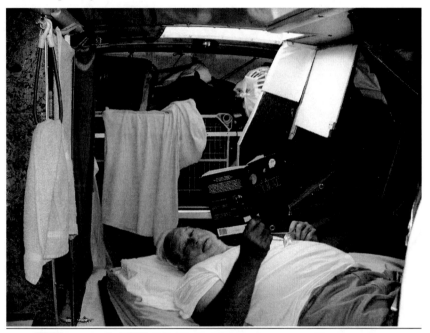

Jim reads while lying on his double bed cabin layout.

James E. Keen

Day #11, Saturday, Jan 29, 2005
Noon Position: 22 deg. 11 min S, 0 deg. 54 min E
528 nautical miles to Saint Helena
Noon-to-Noon Run: 114 nautical miles

＊ ＊ ＊

Bill's Email Dispatch

This is a strange ocean. It has been days since we have seen a bird. Maybe, one school of flying fish a day but no other life. No wind. No waves. No clouds now, so the sun is hot in the day.

Motor, motor, motor . . .

＊ ＊ ＊

We have another beautiful day in paradise with warm temperatures, calm water, and no wind. The motor drones on all day.

On lazy afternoons when I'm off watch, I set up my berth as a double bunk, get out my book, and lie under the open forward hatch where a beautiful breeze and the view of headsails and sky make my day.

Bill has a similar cave in his cabin at the rear of the boat near the main companionway. When sitting in the cockpit on the port side cockpit seat, one is sitting literally inches from his face as he lies in his bunk. I try to keep the Captain happy by remembering to be quiet and not bang on the steel seats with my steel safety harness shackle.

Trinidad Express

Day #12, Sunday, Jan 30, 2005
Noon Position: 20 deg. 52 min S, 0 deg. 25 min W
420 nautical miles to Saint Helena
Noon-to-Noon Run: 108 nautical miles

❧ ❧ ❧

Bill's Email Dispatch

Motor, motor, motor . . .

Notice that "W" after longitude? We have crossed the Greenwich Meridian and are back in the western hemisphere. Still very light wind, and the air is warmer and the sun hotter. In the afternoon we now hide in the shade of the twin genoas. Wind alone will drive the boat at about 3 knots, but we are motoring at 1100 RPM, which boosts the speed to 4.6 knots. We need to maintain 4.2 knots to make anchor down in Saint Helena before sunset on Thursday.

When we were in Richards Bay, the newspapers reported that a woman, somewhere in SA, had been killed by a shark. She was something like 76 years old and went swimming every day, summer and winter. She was an excellent swimmer and well known in the community. One day a Great White got her.

I was cleaning up today and found the newspaper article.

The train ride from Simon's Town to Cape Town starts by going along the shore past beaches crowded with typical families and others enjoying the water, just like a crowded beach in NC. The article shows a picture of a man with binoculars standing on a hill high overlooking the beaches.

(Quote from the newspaper article)

"Abraham Saboe keeps watch for sharks . . . When the lookout spots a shark, he phones the lifesaving club and starts the ball rolling. First,

101

the shark siren is sounded to warn bathers to get out of the water. Next, the warning flag goes up and the lifesaver's boat is launched to patrol the threatened beach."

The community of Vishoek (Fish Hook) is about three miles up the bay from Simon's Town. Vishoek is where the woman was taken by the shark. Just three days before we got there, a Great White was seen about four boat lengths from our slip in the FBYC marina. There was a lot of talk about it at the yacht club.

South Africans boat in the most treacherous waters I have ever experienced, and they swim with sharks. If I could just figure it out, it says something significant about the national character.

⚡ ⚡ ⚡

Bill leads church service in the cockpit and then, as usual, we sit in silence or talk afterward. I don't remember much about today's conversation, but it seemed important at the time. Since I've been aboard, we've talked about wives, children, pets, and pet peeves. We have branched out to politics and more academic subjects, but we back off if there is a disagreement.

Most of our other time is filled with boat duties, sleep, or pursuit of personal projects that prompt minimal conversation. Both of us enjoy conversation but thrive on periods of inward reflection or concentration.

Today was the originally planned landfall day at Saint Helena Island, so Bill is unhappy. He knows that we'll have to make up the lost time somewhere, which will probably be less of a planned layover on the island. We might stay only two days instead of the planned five days.

I hope to get more pineapples, oranges, cantaloupes, apples, and other fresh fruit when we arrive. We've been out of fresh food, except oranges, for several days.

Looks like a Thursday landfall.

Day #13, Monday, Jan 31, 2005
Noon Position: 19 deg. 35 min S, 1 deg. 41 min W
315 nautical miles to Saint Helena
Noon-to-Noon Run: 105 nautical miles

🚢　🚢　🚢

<u>Bill's Email Dispatch</u>

In the South Atlantic, the longer the wind does not blow, the calmer the ocean becomes. The ocean is very, very calm.

🚢　🚢　🚢

The motor drones on and on most of the night and day in flat seas. There are rain showers in the area and the temperature is in the upper 80s with high humidity. This is the first day aboard that I have been uncomfortably hot and sweaty.

Bill has been reading tourist literature about Saint Helena Island.

This afternoon he's making bread while I write in my log. He just showed me a foaming cup of yeast. The last batch didn't foam, so he hopes for lighter bread this time. He seems to enjoy making bread.

Western omelets are my favorite meal on the rare occasion when I cook breakfast. It's a way to salvage bell pepper and cheese. I've made omelets on two occasions and used half of our five dozen egg lauder. I worry about eggs spoiling from lack of refrigeration, although we were careful at the market to buy unrefrigerated eggs as they tend to keep longer. As it turns out, I shouldn't have worried, as unrefrigerated eggs kept most of the way across the ocean until one exploded in an orange mess. I threw the rest overboard.

I made pancakes from scratch yesterday, one large and one baby cake each. I spread on Fiji jam and pancake syrup. The boxed UHT apple juice is a nice addition to our breakfast, although it would have been better served ice cold.

I've been trying to use old cans of food and rarely use the new ones. It is fun opening unmarked cans or cans with JAM FUJI written on top with a black marker. Unmarked cans are always a pleasant surprise, and I quickly learn that a can with a fish symbol really is fish.

Bill says, "Just open a can at random and dump it in!"

Day #14, Tuesday, February 1, 2005
Noon Position: 18 deg. 23 min S, 2 deg. 54 min W
215 nautical miles to Saint Helena
Noon-to-Noon Run: 100 nautical miles

✦ ✦ ✦

Bill's Email Dispatch

Calm, very calm.

✦ ✦ ✦

It's been like driving over a featureless desert plain, riding up and over 10- to 15-foot hills. However, the hills are coming to us from the rear on a following sea. As I look behind, the wind-rippled hill advances, then towers over us, and overtakes us. The boat rides up and over the hill as it continues forward to drop into a gully. It's sort of like riding a roller coaster, with the car standing still and the hilly tracks moving forward.

There's been no wind all day and we are motoring, but not fast enough to outrun the advancing hills. Occasionally, we encounter hills that come from the side which causes the boat to begin a rolling motion. Back and forth we roll, seemingly forever. When I'm on watch and a rolling series starts, I shift my weight against each roll to slow it. I succeed in damping the roll but quickly tire of the effort and just let her roll and roll.

We had a bit of excitement a few minutes ago. Bill spotted a school of fish, porpoise we think, splashing over a wide area. I theorize that they are probably surrounding and herding a school of food fish by making frightening splashes, then taking turns eating the scared fish. Jackie and I learned of this behavior among killer whales while on a boat tour off Juneau, Alaska. Do killer whales and porpoise act the same way?

105

This is the level of morning excitement and quite possibly the day.

It's 215 nautical miles to Saint Helena Island and we can hardly wait for landfall, beer, and fresh greens.

About noon, the diesel stops. In the sudden silence, we look at each other in disbelief. We then calmly discuss the possible problem. From the symptoms, it has to be fuel related, the lack of fuel, or damage to the fuel system.

Bill starts tracing the problem and quickly focuses on a bad fuel cutoff switch. It has misbehaved before. He dissembles the switch and finds nothing wrong. He takes it out of the system anyway, so that fuel can flow unrestricted to the diesel. This changes the way we have to shut down the engine but doesn't fix the problem.

Then Bill finds the problem—the day tank is empty.

Advent II has a large main fuel tank down low in the bilge at the keel. A smaller day tank is mounted under the cockpit but above the engine. Gravity takes over, causing fuel to flow unassisted to the engine. Manually refilling the day tank allows us to keep track of fuel usage.

Every four hours, when the engine is running, the day tank has to be manually filled by pumping fuel from the main tank. This morning, I opened the day tank fuel valve, pumped 50 strokes to raise fuel to the day tank, but then forgot to close the valve. The fuel simply ran back downhill into the main tank and, when the day tank emptied, the diesel quit. Bill pumped fuel into the day tank, closed the valve, and purged air from the fuel lines. The diesel started and ran normally.

I had created a problem and a lot of worry for the Captain. However, he is mad at himself for not starting the diagnosis by immediately checking the fuel level in the day tank. He knows that without the use of the diesel engine, our trip will be a lot slower, and maneuvering near land will be a lot more dangerous.

I'm glad that engineer Bill Doar is a competent mechanic and a tolerant man. He is mad at himself for his inefficiency when he should be mad with the loose cannon that caused the problem in the first place.

Day #15, Wednesday, February 2, 2005
Noon Position: 17 deg. 9 min S, 4 deg. 16 min W
108 nautical miles to Saint Helena
Noon-to-Noon Run: 107 nautical miles

🏴 🏴 🏴

Bill's Email Dispatch

A few days ago the wind was from the southeast at about 10 knots. Then the wind speed dropped and we could not sail because the boat speed would be too slow to keep our schedule. Running the engine adds to our speed and we can make a little less than 5 knots. Today there really is no wind. The sea is slick.

There has been an addition to the honorifics. These are items on board that have served with exceptional performance to the point that they seem to have personalities and have been given names. We have Virginia, Shirley, and Windy, and now Leo, the 62-horsepower Vetus diesel engine. He has taken us through the Panama Canal, most of the way to Galapagos, and now, apparently, across the Atlantic. We occasionally mistreat him, but, like a faithful dog, Leo forgives us. All he really wants to do is what he was bred to do, push this boat. In two days I will remove the cover and give the faithful servant the attention he deserves. Good job, Leo.

🏴 🏴 🏴

We motor during the night watches in light winds. The day dawns calm and overcast with rain squalls. Looks like another day of listening to a loud diesel.

Yesterday, I tried fishing with the hand line and succeeded in drowning a Clark Spoon for about an hour. When I pulled in the line, I found that I had caught an orange peel that Bill had thrown overboard. Either fish don't like orange peels or it scared them away.

108

This morning, between rain sprinkles, I put out the hand line. Within three seconds, an 18-inch dolphin hit the line. He jumps off while I try to bring him on board. Other fish strike at the lure, but escape. After a while, I realize I have a fish on the second line and pull in the drowned brother to the fish that I lost.

"Fish for lunch!" is Bill's excited comment.

In the calm cabin, I fry two smallish fish fillets and serve them with canned potato salad and string beans. The fried fish are very pale because I didn't use a flour coating. I decide it would be better to do so next time. Anyway, I learn a lot about cleaning and cooking fish while underway. The physical exertion is good. The fish is tasty and best of all, fresh!

We need landfall. The repair list includes a broken wind speed indicator, non-functioning depth/speed gauge, and a disassembled engine cutoff switch.

We lust for fresh fruit and beer.

Day #16, Thursday, February 3, 2005
Noon Position: 22 deg. 11 min S, 0 deg. 54 min W
Arrival at Saint Helena
Noon-to-Noon Run: 108 nautical miles

🦎 🦎 🦎

Bill's Email Dispatch

Well, we had fresh fish for lunch. Jim caught a dolphin just right for two. We ate it all, fried fish, potato salad, and string beans.

Good job, Jim.

🦎 🦎 🦎

The wind is blowing nicely when I come on watch at midnight and continues to increase throughout my watch. We sail nicely after almost five days of motoring through windless calm seas.

On night watch, with the silvery glow of moonlight, it is very peaceful in the cockpit. On other nights when the moon is new or down, the scene is black with only light from the stars and instruments barely revealing the cockpit. Sometimes the heavens are so bright I can see my shadow from starlight. Then, I stretch and peer around the canvas cockpit cover to see the stars. The splash of the galaxies is incredibly bright, far brighter than when seen on land near artificial light haze. Out here, hundreds of miles from land, it is black as can be, which enhances the glow of the heavens.

I'm not an expert at identifying stars but among the splash of stars in the Milky Way, I can see the Magellanic Clouds, small galaxies that are only visible from the earth's southern hemisphere. I know a bit about them from a colleague who reads profusely while tending our college computer systems. He has told me about texts of ancients that mention the Magellanic Clouds with awe and wonder.

110

Bill calls me at 0630 hours. When I arrive in the cockpit he points at the horizon.

Saint Helena in the clouds under Trysail and Jib poled out to port.

"Land Ho!" he says.

Saint Helena Island does exist.

Throughout the morning the island appears to grow as we approach and sail around the northeast shoreline to the town of Jamestown, on the western side of the island. We are in awe of the huge blocks of rocky shoreline and mountains that rise over 2,400 feet above the ocean. Turks Head, a symmetrical cone with a pointed cylinder on top, looks like a Turk's cap with smooth, nearly vertical sides that fall into the sea.

"And just think. This is the same view that Napoleon saw as he arrived at the island," was all I could think to say.

James E. Keen

Chapter 3

Saint Helena Island:

Isolated Island of Contrasts

We've found the extremely remote island of Saint Helena after sailing over 1,200 miles to the west of South Africa. Believed to be about 15 million years old, the island is only about 47 square miles in size at 10.5 miles by 6.5 miles. It is a heavily eroded volcano summit rising from an ocean depth of 13,858 feet. Queen Mary's Peak is the highest point on the island with an elevation of 6,758 feet. The coastline has deeply eroded valleys and 1,000-foot high cliffs that plunge directly into the sea. Large rugged uninhabited mountains, valleys, and wastelands occupy much of the island. The remainder is divided between cultivated farms, lush pastures, forests, and small rural settlements.

Jamestown, the largest settlement, is located on the west, dry side of the island. The east side is wet, constantly buffeted by humid southeasterly trade winds.

James E. Keen

Our Island Visit

At noon, we drop anchor in the unprotected roadstead in front of Jamestown. Four other cruising yachts are anchored nearby. Another arrives before nightfall. Boats from France, Germany, Sweden, Holland, and the U.S. (us) make an impressive international selection when you consider that each boat has sailed thousands of miles to anchor here. Bill hails the water taxi for a ride ashore. We are ready for a hamburger and beer at Anne's Place.

The Gallows with ropes to swing ashore.

Docking of boats of any size is impossible, as huge ocean swells slam into the unprotected port. A long breakwater holds back the sea and provides an area where a fixed crane is used to hoist cargo ashore from barges (lighters) which transfer cargo from ships safely anchored well offshore. The unloading of people is accomplished at a small wharf where a strange looking pipe railing, like a gallows, supports trapeze ropes that people use to swing ashore or onto the boat. There is a constant danger of a person being crushed by the dancing boat as it grinds against the wharf.

Jamestown: Historic Forts and Hamburgers

Jamestown, Saint Helena Island. Jacob's Ladder is the thin slanted line on hill at Center Right.

From the water taxi, I can see the town cradled between two 600-foot rough brown mountain masses. Jamestown is a splash of color that stretches about a mile up the valley. Green trees and blue and red tin corrugated roofs peek from behind the wall of a fort.

James E. Keen

Waterfront with Jacob's Ladder in background.

With a relatively calm sea, we bypass the gallows to step ashore from the water taxi without incident. The 200-yard walk to the village is along the waterfront dock, over the dry moat bridge, through a sallyport in the fortress wall into a different world—where time measurement seems different. The bridge and stone archway are the only access onto the island.

For 350 years, guns have pointed outward through these walls in defense of the island. In some places higher on the mountainside, the smoothbore cannons have been removed and WWII rifled guns installed. Just off the dock, along with a junked bulldozer, crane, and several rusted trucks, is a pile of cannons, old and newer, rusty and forgotten.

116

Sallyport through the castle wall looking seaward.

The Castle, the present island administrative center and former governor's town home, is directly behind the fort and adjacent to Castle Garden. Castle Square is used for parking and maneuvering at the start of Main Street as it continues up the hill and valley to bisect the town. The Castle, garden, and Saint James Anglican Church overlook the square, as does a fast food takeout restaurant and a wholesale food warehouse.

Our first stop is at the Castle cashier to change our U.S. dollars into Saint Helena pounds. We can't use our Visa cards because of a communications outage and are limited to the cash we have on hand. We find that US$100 gives us only SHP49 (Saint Helena pounds) which has parity with the British Pound Sterling. The customs office is located in the police station along with the immigration office.

James E. Keen

All the officials, *Saints* as island residents are called, are pleasant, very hospitable, and complete the entry paperwork quickly.

We walk up the hill of Main Street to the Visitor Center. A shade tree has become a local hangout for elderly *Saints* just passing the time. They observe our every move but are pleased and friendly when we stop for a chat.

Jamestown Main Street looking seaward.

In the Visitor Center, a clerk makes arrangements for a guided sightseeing tour of the island, and a visit to Longwood Home, the exile residence of Napoleon. With the tour set for tomorrow, our business is finished. We pause to examine themed exhibits.

In the history exhibit, we find the island was discovered on May 21, 1502, by a Spanish navigator in service of Portugal. This date is the feast day of Saint Helena, mother of the Roman emperor Constantine, so the island name honors that day.

European ships bound for the East Indies began to call for replenishments. In 1659, the English East India Company took possession of the island, a first governor was appointed, and rule by the company lasted until 1834.

In the 1666 aftermath of the Great Fire of London, a group of the homeless became settlers on Saint Helena Island. The island was often called the lost county of England.

In 1672, the Dutch captured the island, only to have it recaptured by the English in 1673. At that time, over half of the population was imported Asian slaves. In 1806, measles was brought from Cape Town and many inhabitants died. Between 1826 and 1836 most slaves were freed.

In 1659, a fort was built on James Bay. The surrounding settlement became the town of Jamestown, named after the Duke of York (later James II).

Charles Darwin, in his ship Beagle, visited Saint Helena Island in 1836 while returning from a trip to the Pacific.

Termites were imported when a Brazilian slave ship was salvaged. Island structures have been ravaged by the pest, with Jamestown Castle requiring a complete rebuild in 1860.

We move on to the exile exhibit and find that the extreme remoteness of the island is ideal for prisoners. Napoleon was confined at Longwood from October 1815, until his death in May 1821. A large garrison of troops was stationed on Saint Helena to prevent his rescue or escape, constant naval patrols were begun, and Ascension Island was occupied to prevent being used in a rescue attempt.

In 1890, Dinuzulu and his entourage were exiled to the island for six years after he leads the Zulu Army against the British in 1883-84. Again, from 1900 to 1902, the island was used to house over 6,000

Boer prisoners of war who camped on Broad Bottom and Deadwood Plain.

In the economy exhibit, we find the island fortunes surged with the influx of troops and costly improvements of defenses that were made during the times of exile. Following the death of Napoleon in 1821, the economy crashed. The East India Company resumed control of the island but went bankrupt in 1834. The island became a British Crown Colony.

In 1869, with the opening of the Suez Canal and the introduction of steam power for ships, sea routes changed and Saint Helena Island declined as a port of call. The island that enjoyed hundreds of vessel visits annually saw a huge reduction in visits. Once more, the island became isolated from the world economy.

In the early part of the 20th century, the island was almost entirely dependent on flax farming. New Zealand flax was planted and used in the manufacture of rope and string until flax demand almost disappeared with the development of cheaper and better substitutes. Although attempts have been made to remove the plant, large patches still grow wild on the island and are considered a pest.

Ascension Island became a communications center, an international airport, and a regional air traffic center. Saint Helena workers gained employment there, and prosperity returned as wages of *Saints* were sent home.

Small-scale tourism, the export of fish, and a limited production of coffee, provide the economic engine of the island today. The collection of customs duties, wharf fees, and the sale of the popular island postage stamps to collectors provide some revenue.

Less than a third of the island is suitable for farming small crops and raising domestic animals. There are no minerals and virtually no industry, except for the timber harvest and local fish harvests that are salted and dried, or frozen for export.

Perennial high levels of imports have caused a large island deficit that results in frequent substantial grants from the United Kingdom. Grants now provide two-thirds of the island budget.

In the island governance exhibit, we find that Saint Helena Island is part of a British Overseas Territory that also includes Ascension Island and Tristan de Cunha. Each island is administered by a British-appointed governor. On Saint Helena, the governor administers island affairs.

The people are a mixture of Portuguese, Dutch, French, English, Malay, Goanese, Madagascan, East Indian, African, Chinese, Boer, and American. The population of about 4,000 people has a reputation for being friendly and lives up to the reputation. During long periods of unemployment on the island, citizens emigrate to nearby countries. Large populations of expat *Saints* reside on Ascension Island, Falkland Islands, the United Kingdom, and South Africa.

Jamestown is the only port for the island and without an airport, the only access to the island for people or goods is by the monthly supply boat, RMS Saint Helena (Britain's last royal mail ship), or by private yacht. Here is a modern society, whose standards are as good as any in the world, which exists in an isolated time warp. The people are born, live, and die relatively untouched by an outside world that has little, but increasing, meaning for them. Satellite TV has just been installed in a few houses on the island, bringing in a barrage of news and culture of the world. Otherwise, the supply ship brings fresh fruit, domestic supplies, a few tourists, and the locals who have been working on Ascension Island. The ship leaves, taking away the previous batch of tourists and a few *Saints,* leaving the island once more without outside transportation. As in in the past century, travel is again measured in months, not hours, yet, it is a modern society.

The town of Jamestown houses about 800 of the 4,000 island residents. Half Tree Hollow and Saint Paul's are larger settlements, while others choose to live in Longwood and clusters of homes scattered about the island.

There are 52 miles of narrow, hilly, and curvy roadways with a 30 mph speed limit. Two long sloping uphill roads carved into the mountainsides on either side of Jamestown are connected to the high central plain.

* * * * * *

We retracing our steps to the square and enter Castle Garden, a formal flower garden shaded by stout trees that have to be hundreds of years old. We find Anne's Place nestled in a back corner of the garden, a wooden deck sheltered by neighboring buildings. There are several unoccupied tables and one table occupied by a young family with two girls. After a look at the menu board, we place our order through the building window.

Anne's Place, one of ten public eateries on Saint Helena, is famous for the atmosphere, decorations, U.S.-style grill food, and, of course, cold beer! The deck is covered by blue tarps to form a ceiling, with huge ship flags suspended underneath. Ships' burgees, signed by sailors who have visited Anne's Place over the years, drape around the edges to create a colorful frill. Pictures of ships, yachts, and visiting crew members are displayed on the walls while a recycled orange ice cooler on a table holds several scrapbooks. Former visitors have signaled their approval of Anne's food and hospitality, with notes, lengthy stories, photos, and signatures on scrapbook pages. It is fascinating to look at familiar sailor names in the books that have visited and written about their travels.

Cold Castle beer and cheeseburgers arrive for two hungry sailors. After our initial order at the window, Anne's son attends to our needs and we talk about life on the island. We meet the real Anne referred to in pictures and comments from the scrapbooks dating back to the 1960s. We talk to the family at a nearby table who are meeting their first Americans.

Properly fed, we make our way back to the water taxi and Advent II. It is time for well-deserved rest.

122

Day #17, Friday, February 4, 2005
Saint Helena Island

Longwood: Napoleon's Exile Home

I open my bunk into a double and sleep under the open hatch, until that is, the rain comes. It is hugely relaxing not to be ruled by four-hour watches and the obnoxious ten-minute timer.

In the morning drizzle, we scurry about the boat preparing to take on water and fuel. The deck jugs of fuel and water are dumped into the ship's tanks so that we can use the empty jugs for transport. With time getting short to meet our tour guide, we leave the empty water and fuel jugs on deck and flag down a water taxi for the ride ashore.

Donald, our day tour driver, meets us at the wharf. He is roughly my height and weight with a rugged dark completion, sun-wrinkled skin, and a receding hairline. His dark blue shorts and collar t-shirt looks nice for the occasion. We take off our foul weather gear as we climb into Donald's ride—a beautiful, clean, bright red Range Rover sedan. Donald drives up the wharf and over the moat bridge into Castle Square, then up Main Street to the Visitor Center. There he takes the left fork onto Napoleon Street to the start of Side Path Road, a steep incline up the side of the mountain.

To go anywhere on the island from Jamestown, you must drive up one of two steep roadway inclines, Side Path Road and Ladder Hill Road, to gain the six hundred foot mountain plateau. Nineteenth-century Chinese work gangs carved the roadways from the mountain and built the massive stone road supports. They also built the Jamestown Entrance Fort, Ladder Hill Fort, and many other structures on the island.

We crest the mountain in clearing weather and drive past residential communities scattered along the road. Houses are oriented to gain the maximum view of the valley and sea, with some houses having rear service entrances facing the public road. Concrete block, with stucco finish, and colorful corrugated steel roofing are the building materials of choice. Gutters catch rainwater for drinking, and most houses have solar hot water heaters and a rooftop hot water tank. Satellite television antennas decorate a few houses, a new gadget that only arrived two years earlier.

The roads are Macadam, rock splashed with tar, and about one and a half lanes wide. When meeting other cars, one car pulls into a passing spot that is usually just a wide area in the road. People drive sensibly, but on the wrong side, quite British-like!

Remnants of flax plantations and barren land dominate much of the island. Vegetation has been ravaged by herds of wild goats and pigs that elude capture in the rugged terrain. Only a few areas of level ground exist and are known as Longwood, Deadwood, Broad Bottom, and Prosperous Bay plains.

Early for our appointment, Donald drives past Longwood House, the Saint Helena Golf Club, and the island trash dump, to find a terrific overlook view of Turk's Cap. It stands in the distance, framed this time by the sea.

"That's where they plan to build the new airport and resort," Donald offers, as he points to a hilly glade overlooking the eastern coastline. "Some favor it, others oppose it!"

We all agree that building an airport will forever change the isolated, unspoiled character of Saint Helena Island. An airport will bring an unprecedented volume of tourists that will result in modernization. Changes will provide a badly needed economic boost, at a price of the loss of solitude, and the unspoiled, unworldly pace of life. As of early 2012, the airport project has not been started.

* * * * * *

Back at the parking area, near the front entrance of Longwood, a small wooden white sign reads, "LONGWOOD HOUSE, MAISON DE

NAPOLEON" in crude black stencil lettering. I have read a bit about choosing Longwood as a place of exile.

News of Napoleon's exile arrived by fast sailboat, just six days ahead of the fleet bringing Napoleon and his party to Saint Helena. Island leaders had to quickly choose a place of incarceration for the

Longwood House crudely lettered sign.

former ruler of France. The best house on the island was Plantation House, the country home of the island governor. It would serve the purpose well, located on easily defended and isolated land. But they decided against the elegant home, instead choosing a dilapidated farmhouse in one of the wettest, windiest, and dampest locations on the island. Longwood was a farm house that had been a stable, renovated into a country house, then left in disrepair.

Napoleon was temporarily quartered at The Briars, the Balcombe family estate, sited in a nearby lovely valley. He and his family party lived for six weeks in the estate summer pavilion, a one-room outbuilding, while repairs were made to Longwood House.

Our guide arrives, a friendly South African man who meets us for a personalized tour of the restored historic French treasure. He confirms that Longwood and the surrounding plot of land are owned and recognized by the French as their territory. He answers questions about himself first. He had taken a holiday on Saint Helena Island, fell in love with the place, and moved here. Although he looks classically French, he is South African.

Longwood House, Napoleon's home on Saint Helena Island

He leads us to a four-foot high rock wall surrounding the house and garden, through a green wooden picket gate, and past a wooden guard house. It is painted green with a peaked shingled roof.

Flower beds surround the nine-room farmhouse with drifts of Everlasting Daisies, day lilies, and other colorful flowers that sway in the wind. The garden had its genesis in Napoleon's personally sketched design which includes a sunken path and gazebo. The dictator took part in its physical creation by joining the house staff in the digging and planting. Seed packets were sent to Napoleon by the wife of a prominent London politician. She disapproved of his exile and defied convention and her husband by sending Everlasting Daisies and other seeds. Offspring of those original flowers are now scattered about the island.

Stunted pines and tall majestic Norfolk Island Pines accent the house. Longwood Home is a single-story, T-shaped stucco building with the front entrance at the bottom of the tee. A two-story series of auxiliary buildings are around back in a courtyard, along with stable buildings. The French tricolor flies on a flagpole next to the front porch that is enclosed with an airy green lattice wall with an arched entrance.

The white stucco building is accented with dark green shutters and contrasting painted corner quoins. A light red shingled roof covers the entrance, while the rest of the structure has light and dark green roof shingles and dark green painted chimneys. Window frames are painted a rich brown, which contrasts nicely with the green shutters, in a manner similar to homes in France.

A massive palm tree, at least 4 feet in diameter, but only about 20 feet tall, snuggles close by one of the garage buildings. The whole scene looks like a farm house with an overachieving flower garden.

We follow a garden path along a low green wooden picket fence to the front entrance. An entry room is furnished with an enormous pool table dominating the center, a four drawer chest, a writing table, a black stone fireplace and mantel with mirror, and twin antique globes in the opposite corners–one celestial and one world. The walls are painted deep green with white door and baseboard trim setting off the dark wood floors. Lighted wall sconces illuminate paintings and the room.

This room served as the audience room. During his long illness, the pool table was removed so Napoleon could receive the many curious visitors. It is reported that Napoleon used the pool table only as a desk to spread out his correspondence for reading and sorting.

The next room, the deathbed room, has a fireplace flanked by benches with dark green upholstery and Napoleon's tented lounge and deathbed on the opposite wall. A bronze death mask of Napoleon, on a pillow as a centerpiece, sits on a small round table in the center of the room. The walls are covered by cream flowery wallpaper, a reproduction of the original, with white painted chair railings, white baseboard, and more dark wood floors. An enormous cut glass chandelier hovers over Napoleon's mask, lighting the room and the bronze.

The deathbed, the only really interesting piece in the room, is a chaise lounge that is covered with a green cloth peaked tent, gathered with a bronze finial. The tent was used as mosquito netting. It's hard to visualize the very small dictator lying there, receiving endless visitors, reflecting on the past: lingering until death.

Trinidad Express

* * * * * *

Bill summarized Napoleon's life in one of his earlier email dispatches.

🐝   🐝   🐝

Napoleon was a brilliant army officer when the First French Republic was unraveling, a hero because of his success on the battlefield. He took advantage of weakness to step in and take over. He was neither a royalist nor a Republican, but a pragmatist and what we call now a benevolent dictator. The innovations he instituted in France, such as in education, civil service, medicine, the judicial system, military and police forces, have been the basis of France even until now.

But Napoleon became ambitious and decided to take over all of Europe. After conquering all of continental Europe he had himself made an emperor. He needed naval superiority to invade Britain, but Lord Nelson sank Napoleon's fleet at Trafalgar; however, he still had his army and continued gobbling up territory until Wellington won the battle of Waterloo.

Napoleon was exiled to the island of Elba in the Mediterranean, escaped, ruled France again for 100 days, was re-defeated, and was then exiled to Saint Helena.

While he lived, the British were paranoid he would escape again. He was under constant surveillance, all contact with the outside world was monitored, and army officers escorted him whenever he left the Longwood grounds.

Napoleon conquered countries, sacrificed millions on battlefields, and caused untold suffering. In the end, he was confined to the small island with only his family and trusted associates, with an English military ensuring his exile. What an appropriate punishment for such a man. He lay here in obscurity, without the adulation which he was accustomed, as his life drained away with age and illness.

🐝   🐝   🐝

We follow beautiful, antique wide plank flooring into other rooms. As I admire the floors, our guide explains, "These floors are reasonable replacements. The house had rotten floors that let in the rats and damp."

The wallpaper oozed gaseous arsenic from the paper dyes. Arsenic was an ingredient in rat poison and used in hair care products during that period.

"It should be no surprise that a modern analysis of Napoleon's hair has given rise to the theory that Napoleon was poisoned. Not so!" squeaked the frail guide. "Napoleon was much too heavily attended in his final days for someone to poison him. He most likely died of stomach cancer, as did his other relatives!"

Other rooms are less interesting but filled with rather unique antique furniture and a period metal bathtub. The kitchen is crude but standard for the period. Our guide continues to recite facts and stories of the times as we are expertly ushered out into the rear courtyard.

The hour-long tour ends at the ubiquitous gift shop that had been carved out of a stable building. We spend the requisite time browsing among the kitsch without purchasing anything. In retrospect, I should have bought one of those felt Napoleon hats, so I could wear it for night watches—only Bill would see.

Back in Donald's car, we drive toward the south end of the island.

Plantation House: Turtles on the Lawn

"A stop at The Plantation House is a must," says Donald. He is referring to the 1791 island Governor's home, reportedly one of the best architectural structures on the island.

We follow the winding road past rolling pastures of the Saint Paul's settlement to enter a glade where a huge house stands among stately trees. Passing the front driveway, we take a side lane beside a chain link

Plantation House, Saint Helena Island.

fence with green posts. Donald stops the car at the kissing gate, a simple wire gate in the fence.

We walk onto a large sloping and closely mowed parched paddock (lawn). A depressed level area has a tennis court that is surrounded by more chain link and green posts. The mansion sits at the top of the lawn on a terrace.

Plantation house is two stories of yellow-green painted brick, topped with a mansard roof of gray slate. The nicely proportioned portico entry has six large windows, three windows on each side. The second story windows are identical, seven windows that give a pleasing balance to the structure. The windows have light gray shutters that match the roof while the brick corner quoins look almost like ladders and give the building strength. Decorative gutters run down the sides of the corners so as not to deface the elegant brick back facade.

The entry portico has a simple doorway with matching side floor-to-ceiling windows. A fan-shaped window is above the plain glass door. A nicely proportioned gable tops the portico giving the structure a sunroom appearance. This is obviously the back of the house as the front would surely have much more ornamentation.

A terrace runs the length of the building, but we cannot see it from our vantage point on the lower lawn. The chain link fence runs along the front of the terrace to complete the lawn closure, the turtle pen. A gate and simple concrete steps lead down to the lawn decorated with the unused tennis court.

Nobody is around for our meeting of the turtles. Bill and I thread our way through the brown grass, dodging the horse-sized dung deposits, to find well-preserved Galapagos tortoises lounging in the warm sun. I approach the largest creature, Jonathan they call him. He's reportedly the oldest tortoise in the world. I crouch about five feet from its nose and look it straight in the eye. He stares back without any sign of acknowledgment.

I think of how I used to do the same with my dog Sandy. She would stare blankly as I faced her, trying to stare her down. After a moment, she would wag her tail slowly and then burst into joyous greeting as she nuzzled my face.

Jonathan just stares back. I keep my distance as I know these animals have strong bites. An ancient looking rough scaly skin covers

his neck and chest below the nicely shaped shell. Two large scale-covered flipper feet are firmly planted on the ground to raise the turtle for movement.

I count six diamond shaped plates around the shell with a single plate on top. The shell has heavily rolled edges and covers him completely except for about a third of the

Jim meeting Jonathan

underside in the front. The long thick neck, at least five inches in diameter, ends with cold black eyes, a wickedly dangerous looking mouth, and a flat black nose. The face looks somewhat like a snake but has a curious look, sort of like he is smiling.

I go over to where Bill is looking at three more tortoises, Emma, Myrtle, and Fredrika in a muddy patch in front of a small doghouse-like shelter. These reptiles are much smaller females, contented to munch on the longer parched grass. A fifth specimen, David, is some distance away toward the house.

A well-kept garden, below the fence at the lower end of the lawn, is devoted to producing food for the turtles with any excess being used by the Governor's family and islanders. I can see the sea beyond and a magnificent view of the cloud-shrouded land to the south.

We drive south on the lane and find the main road. Farms appear in the distance surrounded by outbuildings and pastures with isolated wild patches of flax and woodland.

Donald stops at an overlook and we get out, stretching our legs along the roadside. In the distance, past the farms, the land drastically changes to barren hills and rugged ravines, obviously ravaged by the wild herds of animals left by earlier settlers. In this wild terrain, herds elude capture and eradication.

Several towering monoliths, volcanic dykes or pitons, are scattered among the hilly barrens—a larger piton just beyond the farm with a smaller one toward the sea.

Lot and Lot's Wife under low clouds.

"They're called Lot and Lot's Wife," Donald volunteers. "Others are called The Sisters."

I marvel at the sight, musing at how high the land must have been over the top of the upended dyke. Scientists tell us that the land eroded over eons leaving the exposed volcanic spires. It boggles the mind! Those eons of time and the gigantic forces make me feel so very small and insignificant.

Donald's Rover takes us to a forested area where the road pierces the trees like a tunnel. The bright sunlight dims to cool shadows as we ride toward the distant end. Abruptly, the scene changes as cattle graze on steep hillsides prompting Bill and me to joke like drunken sailors about left-side and right-side cattle. We laugh, but Donald tends to his driving without breaking a smile. He must think we're crazy.

Residential neighborhoods crowd the road, with a view to the north at the head of the ravine that leads down to Jamestown. Nestled below is the Prince Andrew School, standing silently amid sports fields and parking lots. There seems to be nobody about. It must be class time!

James E. Keen

Ladder Hill Fort: History, With a View

Past the school and a little to the west, the valley continues in a gentle slope down a short distance to the outskirts of Jamestown. Donald pilots us along the high ridge top road overlooking the valley, then past more houses to Ladder Hill Fort, the barracks, and the summit of Jacob's Ladder.

Jamestown harbor with boats anchored in open ocean

We tour the fort and the fortified stone barracks that housed English soldiers during years of occupation of Saint Helena. The barracks museum has empty stone rooms that look very uncomfortable. There is, however, a commanding vista of the ocean from south along the mountain, straight out toward the west, and north to the mountain on the other side of Jamestown. The harbor lies six hundred feet below, immediately to the northwest. I think I can identify Advent II in the gaggle of boats anchored in the roadstead.

The curving form of Jamestown Bay washes up against the town breakwater. I see the wide wharf work surface where a fixed crane operates to unload barges that haul cargo when ships anchor farther out in the bay. No ships are anchored there today, and the wharf is quiet. Cars are parked along the seawall to relieve parking congestion on nearby Castle Square.

136

Along the shoreline of the mountain, on the other side of town, is a narrow road on a thin strip at the bottom of a sheer cliff. At the far end, at the pedestrian wharf, I can see the steps leading down to the seaside concrete dock where the gallows await to hang pirates or assist passengers to board their boat or swing onto land.

Jamestown between two mountains with interior access roads.

Barges, used to transport goods from ships, sit upended on the concrete dock after having been lifted ashore by a mobile crane. Stored shipping containers sit idle in a yard scrunched next to the sheer mountainside. Small white buildings with blue corrugated tin roofs house the Saint Helena Yacht Club. I remember how deserted and unused the club buildings looked when we passed earlier. I even peeked into the soiled bath and laundry facilities. Yuck!

From where I'm standing, the opposite mountain appears the same height and a twin of this mountain, with exposed rock that forms sheer cliffs above the harbor. The few small buildings that are visible on the far mountaintop include a smaller companion fort and communications building with large antennas. The access road up the mountain to these facilities is much more rugged and meant for utility vehicles, not the general public.

Jamestown Fort, with the dry moat and a few antique cannon aimed toward the bay, lies between the quay and the shimmering blue community swimming pool. Umbrellas, waiting to pamper guests, are scattered around a concrete lounging area. A higher seawall, behind the swimming pool, has an arched access that leads to Jamestown Castle.

A single central road and moat bridge lead from the dock to the town square. Near the bridge is a shed that probably contains changing rooms and toilets for the public tennis courts. The green playing surface with white marking lines is surrounded by a lounging area with more umbrellas.

I can see Castle Square. Rectangular buildings with light blue corrugated tin rooftops crowd about. Cars fill most all the clearly marked parking spaces around the perimeter, leaving the central area for maneuvering around the start of Main Street. Cyril's Fast Food is next to the arch. I remember seeing a crowd milling around a service window when we passed this morning. The back of a wholesale food store is visible as is Castle Garden where a green patch of trees hides Anne's Place.

A light blue corrugated tin roof covers Saint James Anglican Church: built in 1774, it's reportedly the oldest Anglican Church in the southern hemisphere. With its arched church windows and tall clock tower next to the square, it has walls of gray stucco and few adornments, except for short pointed spires at the corners of the clock tower.

Other light blue and red corrugated tin roofed buildings are scattered up the valley in a slender arrowhead shape that points toward the interior of the island. As I look to the east up Main Street, it widens into twin driving lanes with angled parking in between, then splits into twin roads at the Visitor Center. The north fork, Side Path Road, is the road we took earlier today and leads up the mountain to the high central interior plain. The right fork leads to the island school complex. Yet another road, Ladder Hill Road, turns off and up the mountain where switchbacks soften the climb to land just behind where I'm standing.

Jacob's Ladder: A Long Way Down

Jacob's Ladder viewed from 600-ft. high Ladder Hill.

The ladder, built in 1829, is an incredible nine hundred foot long stairway. It has six hundred ninety nine steps that descend the almost forty-five degrees, six-hundred-foot high hillside to land in Jamestown at the edge of Castle Square. Built originally to haul manure up to farms on the elevated plane, it was later used by the military as an inclined plane to haul supplies on carts up to the barracks. Horses operated a capstan that pulled carts up the plane, carrying as much as four tons each.

The steps, maybe an afterthought built for the convenience of the residents, are an awkward eleven inches high when the normal modern step is about eight inches. The three foot wide stairway is flanked by flat concrete tracks where the wheels of the supply cart once rode. A pipe handrail looks like a modern addition to the stairway, made in the name of safety.

The stairs present a challenge to younger residents. A timed run up the steps is held annually and attracts participants from around the world. Older residents prefer an alternate forty-five minute road ride into town along the switchback Ladder Hill Road.

Some time later, at the Visitor Center and again at a convenience store, I quiz *Saints* about climbing Jacob's Ladder. Folks easily respond with stories of how they had to descend the ladder to go to school and climbed it again later to go home. Each tells a classic walk-to-school story that probably has some truth in it.

A photo on the wall at the Visitor Center shows boys with feet on one iron railing and back and arms on the other, sliding down the stairway railings. They must have had trouble explaining to their mothers about worn-out pants legs and shirt sleeves. The photo caption reports the long narrow incline plane would, "Break your heart going up and break your neck coming down."

At night, with lights every fifteen feet all the way to the top, the incline looks like a beautiful stairway to heaven. In other places, they would light the stairway to give the city a unique identity to attract tourists. On Saint Helena, they did it because it is beautiful.

* * * * * *

We endure the hair-raising descent as Donald negotiates the one-lane, very busy Ladder Hill Road. We stop in a wide spot, yielding to the upward bound school bus and other traffic as required by law. Our tour ends at Castle Square where another visit to Anne's Place nets a Dagwood sandwich with a cheeseburger, ham, and egg on a large roll. Of course, we have Castle Beer that is cold and wonderful.

Our eventful day ends early as I collapse in my luxurious double bunk for another ten hours of sleep in a softly rocking bed.

Day #18, Saturday, February 5, 2005
Saint Helena Island

Preparations for Getting Underway

A new day in our paradise brings rain and the wind that whips off nearby cliffs. Early morning rain, followed by clearing weather, seems to be the norm. After a slow start, Bill works on departure preparations while I clean up and stay out of the way.

Bill announces that it is time to climb the mast. Sailing gear tends to chafe easily causing concern about the failure of critical items. Frequent gear inspection, including going aloft, is the cure. Wearing his professional safety gear, and having me belay him with a halyard, Bill climbs to the mast top while checking rigging as he goes. He finds the cups on the wind speed sensor flopping uselessly; our wind speed instrument now permanently out of action. Otherwise, Bill pronounces the rigging sound and worthy of another ocean passage.

We rest after the mast climbing exertion, and I begin to think again about a piece I have been writing about World Cruising Yachties (WCY). I've had a bit of time now to observe this creature: at the FBYC docks and bar, the CTYC docks in a brief meeting with Bill's friends, and at meetings with yachties around the harbor and onshore here at Saint Helena. Here's what I have written.

* * * * * *

World Cruising Yachties

People who choose to cruise the world in a personal sail/power vessel are an eclectic bunch and are a challenge to categorize.

Cruising boat crews are mostly couples. The majority is 50 to 70 years of age, and many have cruised for ten years or more. Most of the remaining boats have all male crews (usually three or more) while a few boats have a one person crew. I've yet to meet an all female crew or female singlehander, although I know they exist.

Many WCY (World Cruising Yachties) have advanced professional degrees while others have educations that are above their country's average. A thirst for knowledge and travel generally flows from their educational experiences. They choose to be ruled daily by the sea, rather than a government.

WCY are a select financial fraternity, largely due to the initiation fee; a world cruising boat can cost $100,000, an amount that can double or triple. Cruising costs can add an additional $20,000 to $30,000 or more annually, and don't forget boat maintenance and insurance fees of $5,000 to $10,000 plus.

A significant percentage of WCY have inherited wealth, with boat and cruising costs representing a smallish proportion of their holdings. Similar cruisers are entrepreneurs who will say, "Well, I sold the business back in 1995 and have just been doing it ever since." These cruisers are only taking a tangent in life and not adopting a lifestyle change.

The initiation fee leaves lots of potential world cruisers tied to the dock. Inventive skippers sell their homes and cars to purchase and equip the boat. Precious little cash remains for cruising. Others retain shore assets but use them as collateral for a boat loan. Boat payments dry up needed income. Unwisely, these cruisers often sail naked of boat insurance, thereby placing their primary asset in jeopardy.

WCY generally have less net worth than their shore-side peers. Cruisers pay a large opportunity cost of not working while accumulating exotic memories. Meanwhile, shore bound peers accumulate wealth.

So, the bottom line on finances is that WCY is divided among two categories: the wealthy with little financial concerns and others whose assets are tied up in a boat. The financially challenged cruiser sails frugally, mainly on unearned fixed income. Some choose to find limited work along the way to subsidize their cruising habit. Nonetheless, compared to a general world society, WCY are relatively wealthy citizens.

American, Australian, and European nationalities dominate the WCY clan, although cruisers come from disparate countries. I have not seen Asian or middle-eastern countries represented among their numbers and although many South African cruisers tour the world, few are black.

Surprisingly, WCY speak the world nautical language of English well, even though it's obviously their second language. Regardless of their nationality, most WCY spoke to me in English. I wonder if they view Americans as language challenged or were just being courteous.

WCY wear khaki or jean shorts and favor open-toe sandals in an attempt to beat the heat. Dress shirts and blouses are worn ashore with knit shirts seldom seen and t-shirts mostly avoided in public. I've already said that Bill chooses to wear recycled white cotton business dress shirts ashore in some sort of reference to his past professional life. Worn without an undershirt, his dress shirts are cool and look nice, in spite of occasional rust stains and dirty spots.

Some male yachties favor the spiffy-looking Canadian Tilley yachting hat; however, any hat that offers good cool sun protection is used. I chose a floppy hat for overall ease and comfort but would like to have my baseball cap back, even though it would let my ears burn. Women sometimes choose a visor cap like those favored on the golf course.

WCY learn to avoid the noon tropical sun, yet still have dry, wrinkled, ruddy skin from exposure to the elements. Hair is often sun-bleached, windswept, short, and white is the normal color, more a result of age than worry.

Most WCY men have a beard. Shaving on a moving boat is dangerous and a bother. One exception is a 30-something cruising couple I met just yesterday and like to call Ken and Barbie in reference to their gold-plated boat and well-scrubbed personal hygiene. The clean-shaven, spiffy man never had a hair out of place and she wore spotless sundresses with brightly painted toenails sparkling in her sandals.

The norm is a genuine friendliness. A typical chat proceeds from "hellos" to "how many days?" to determining first names. Last names are only for close friends. Then, you talk about the home port, nationality, boat models, children and family, and news from mutual cruising friends. A genuine interest is evident, often growing into fondness. One exception was the braggadocio lawyer from Alaska that I met at Simon's Town. Bill chided me, "Remember, he possesses the skill to get here by boat, so just forgive his little faults."

Bill reminds me that all people who sail to remote places are accepted into the WCY fraternity, regardless of sailing in a $1,000,000 catamaran or a $20,000 Westsail. The fact that they are capable of sailing to such places earns respect and the right to be called a World Cruising Yachtie.

True friendships develop with repeated meetings along favored routes. As a fiercely independent bunch, WCY tends to choose their own departure date, regardless of their friends' schedules. If a later meeting takes place, all is well. If no meeting takes place, so be it. However, as friendships blossom, WCYs will spend their waking hours with newfound acquaintances. That is, until their true cruising nature surfaces and they must move on, leaving the more sedentary behind.

WCYs prefer to party on the beach or on one of their boats. Potluck meals are common, with sailors bringing exotic dishes made from recipes collected around the world. Mainstream restaurants are avoided as expensive tourist traps, but pubs or local fisherman's bars are favored for local outings.

WCYs are true gypsies, if just so for a short period. They are free-spirited and thoughtful, fiercely interested, and protective of the environment. They are truly an eclectic bunch.

Trinidad Express

* * * * * *

We flag down the water taxi and go ashore with empty fuel and water jugs and bags of soiled laundry. While Bill goes off to change money to buy food and fuel, I do laundry.

The yacht club bath facility contains rude toilet and shower facilities that, although surrounded by white tile, convey a sense of uncleanness. There is a two-sink laundry arrangement: one for soapy water and the other for rinse, I surmise. I start by soaking my huge laundry load and Bill's three or four shirts. It's not that Bill is dirty, he just knows how to conserve clean clothes, or so he says. I wash the clothes, transfer them to the clear rinse water, hand wring everything, and stuff the wet bundles into a bag for drying on the boat. Bill returns and assigns my next chore of buying food. He will buy fuel and then haul the fuel and clean, but wet, laundry to the boat.

* * * * * *

Bill and Normandie had problems around the world finding cheap canned meats. The existing larder contains lots of beans, rice, pasta, and fish; however, there is little canned meat for our one-pot meals.

I find the wholesale house right on Castle Square. They sell case lots of canned goods and paper supplies, but it is not a cheap store. I buy cases of canned hamburger, beef chunks, Spam, beef stew, and a dozen packages of English cream crackers similar to our saltines, only larger. Now I have greater one-pot meal choices for the next five weeks but I am sixty-two Saint Helena pounds poorer (US$120).

At the wharf, I fill the water jugs and load them and the groceries onto the water taxi. It's not an easy job since the taxi boat is in constant motion from the ocean swell. I time my motions with the swell and place one jug at a time into the boat at the height of the swell. I am careful not to get crushed between the boat and dock. Waiting for the next swell, I load another and then another. After I finish, I use an overhead rope to swing my bulk aboard. I secure the hastily loaded jugs and groceries as the water taxi swings round with perfect timing of the swell and we roar toward Advent II.

Bill had indicated early in our planning sessions that we would have a real problem transporting fuel and water in the dinghy. However, being able to haul the heavy jugs by water taxi is wonderful. It costs 1 Saint Helena pound per person per day for the taxi, a real value as we don't have to assemble the folded and stowed dinghy.

* * * * * *

Our boat, with laundry drying in the rigging, has fifty gallons of fuel, ten jugs, on deck for loading into the main tanks, along with a similar number of water jugs. She looks like an unorganized tramp.

We siphon fuel into the main fuel tank, and I chlorinate individual water jugs before dumping them into the main water tanks. Bill changes Leo's oil, replaces the fuel shut-off valve, and works on the balky depth sounder. He declares the sounder dead giving him a tally on electronic repairs of zero for two.

We taxi back ashore so Bill can make our official departure check out while I go to the fuel dock to fill two more fuel jugs and find fresh bread. The fuel dock is closed as are most other stores in town.

Jamestown is similar to many eastern North Carolina towns of fifty years ago in that everyone goes to town on Saturday morning. People visit with their seldom-seen rural neighbors and shop for staples and clothes for the kids. These visits often stretch into the night with some sort of group entertainment happening before everyone heads back home.

On Saint Helena, the same is true, except most shops close early "to go see the kids play at the school athletic field." I do find fresh bread at the only open shop, but fresh fruit is simply unavailable as the twice monthly supply boat has not yet arrived.

After a final walk around to ensure a sea ready deck, Bill announces it is time to weigh anchor. At 1700 hours, I spend a back-breaking fifteen minute workout using the manual windlass to raise one hundred fifty feet of chain and the one hundred ten pound anchor.

Maybe this is why cruisers are slim.

Sailing away from Jamestown.

After spending just two days on Saint Helena Island, rather than the scheduled five days, we sail into the setting sun as porpoises cross our wake.

James E. Keen

Chapter 4

Second Leg: Sailing to Fernando de Noronha

 Day #19, Sunday, February 6, 2005
Noon Position: 15 deg. 26 min S, 6 deg. 58 min W
1,660 nautical miles to Fernando de Noronha
Noon-to-Noon Run: 75 nautical miles

❋ ❋ ❋

Bill's Email Dispatch

We departed Saint Helena, 1700 hours, for Fernando de Noronha off the coast of Brazil, a distance of about 1,660 nautical miles.

It feels good to be sailing again. We had motored so long that it became the norm, but now the wind is light and we are averaging little more than 4 knots. Yesterday at Saint Helena the sky was sunny, but just as we were leaving a cloud rolled in. I thought it was the ubiquitous cloud over all islands, but it was cloudy all night and all today. I guess I could use the drifter, but I don't trust the clouds. There may be too much wind in them.

❋ ❋ ❋

149

It was my second experience sailing from a place that I had learned to love. I stare at the island, converting my new understanding and knowledge of this place into memories.

Although sailing away from Simon's Town was filled with new experiences of rough ocean sailing that is now a blur, sailing away from Saint Helena Island is effortless. We up the anchor without fanfare, motor a few miles, raise sails, and sail into the sunset. My memories crystallize while looking at the receding, vividly detailed scene of forts, mountains, and the town. I watch the island turn from normal green and tan to a purple shadow, to a black haze with lights outlining the community and finally to a faint hint of light on the horizon.

I've developed an optimistic habit of telling people, "I'll be back on my own boat in five years." In my mind, I know that, in all probability, I've looked at Jamestown for the last time.

* * * * * *

Our first day offshore is characterized by winds of unsettled direction, requiring frequent adjustments to Windy and the sails. Even so, we quickly settle into the now familiar seagoing routine, taking up where we left off earlier. I know my role, and Bill is less anxious about my abilities. Maybe I've become more of a WYC.

Today is Bill's birthday. A postcard mounted on a bulkhead had announced both Bill and Normandie's birthdays. I bought some cupcake muffins and birthday cake candles while shopping on Saint Helena, made fishcakes for lunch, lit the cupcake candle, and watched Bill eat his present—the last juicy orange on board. We were unable to find fresh fruit on the island and, it'll be a long slog to the next port. We both eat a muffin—his with a candle, mine without.

We have a lazy afternoon and late church service in the cockpit. The day flows into a new moon dark night and all is well.

Trinidad Express

Day #20, Monday, February 7, 2005
Noon Position: 14 deg. 31 min S, 8 deg. 49 min W
1,537 nautical miles to Fernando de Noronha
Noon-to-Noon Run: 123 nautical miles in 25 hours

✍ ✍ ✍

Bill's Email Dispatch

Very smooth sailing, wing-n-wing, 5.5 knots, overcast and a cool 82 degrees. This is very comfortable sailing.

✍ ✍ ✍

Today is my first twenty-five hour day. Bill changes the clocks to signify entering a new time zone and our crossing of another 15° segment of the earth's surface. We're now only four hours ahead of North Carolina time.

We've had marvelous wind and weather today, the sails flying wing-n-wing with genoa and mainsail. We're scampering along at five to six knots, with easy sailing over a relatively placid sea.

I heat canned, cooked hamburger patties, slice fresh bread, tomatoes, and onions, and then add cheese, mustard, and ketchup for a great meal. Bill said it was the first time he has eaten cheeseburgers in paradise (at sea). The canned hamburgers were caked with grease but look and taste surprisingly good when heated. We can almost imagine we're eating burgers at a local home joint except these burgers do not have lettuce and pickles. The canned meat purchase has brightened meal choices.

Our intellectual conversation today centered on my WCY essay. Bill took me to task on my assumptions about the financial arrangements all cruisers make, essentially telling me I was wrong. I've improved the piece with new financial assumptions. I hope the improved version, the one I presented to you, better captures the essence of the WCY.

Day #21, Tuesday, February 8, 2005
Noon Position: 13 deg. 50 min S, 10 deg. 33 min W
1,428 nautical miles to Fernando de Noronha
Noon-to-Noon Run: 109 nautical miles

❦ ❦ ❦

Bill's Email Dispatch

We are having beautiful, easy sailing. Twin poles fly straight before the wind giving the boat a speed generally in the upper 4s on a calm sea. The temperature is 82 degrees, so we are very comfortable. Sailing is so relaxing.

❦ ❦ ❦

I wake to the sounds of Bill messing about on the deck.

"I should be helping," is my thought as I hop out of the bunk and put on my pants. The morning seas are calm and Advent II is sailing along nicely. As I use a two point hold to zip my fly, the boat does a dip, and I fly head first into Normandie's eight- by ten-inch vanity mirror. I see stars—well actually a big star crack in the mirror. No damage to the head, but the mirror is ruined.

On deck, I note that Bill is unusually relaxed. I realize he hasn't made a list since our Simon's Town departure. Remembering those busy times, I understand the tremendous pressure he must have felt preparing to take a boat offshore for up to ninety days with a greenhorn aboard. Forgetting to buy toilet tissue is an inconvenience but failing to carry enough water can be life threatening.

Bill compensated by making lists.

However, departing Saint Helena was simple. When we had water and fuel aboard, Bill simply said, "Let's go!" Bill was list-less and I was green-less.

152

We have trade wind squalls today. They move fast with just enough water in them to get the deck wet and raise the humidity level. Each squall must be taken seriously as they can contain dangerously high winds. Consequently, the drifter had to be secured with each cloud.

Day #22, Wednesday, February 9, 2005
Noon Position: 14 deg. 31 min S, 8 deg. 49 min W
1537 nautical miles to Fernando de Noronha
Noon-to-Noon Run: 100 nautical miles

🌀 🌀 🌀

<u>*Bill's Email Dispatch*</u>

Another day of lazy sailing with twin poles with speed in the mid-4s to mid-5s. At night the wind slows to around 4 knots. We are very comfortable, and at this rate will get to Fernando de Noronha in 13 days.

🌀 🌀 🌀

When the normal winds return, Bill lets me do the foredeck work as he monitors my progress and takes care of my cockpit duties. Even sailing in calm water, you cannot stand upright on deck without a four point hold. But, to get anything done, you have to release one hand. The key is to slow down and take the time to think about and plan each move.

I furl the genoa, redeploy it on the starboard pole, raise the drifter, deploy it on the port pole, secure the trysail on the main boom, and cover it with the mainsail cover. The complicated deck work takes an hour but would have taken much longer in heavy seas. This was practice on deck for me before we encounter a heavy weather situation. It's hard to imagine standing upright on the foredeck in really bad weather and I hope I never see those conditions.

My ten-minute check reveals a gorgeous sky with puffy clouds at the horizon, a smooth sea, and declining boat speed as the wind is fading. I note a rip in the lower edge of the big genoa and quickly furl the sail before the tear expands.

We now sail along under the drifter alone as I wait for Bill to rouse from his nap to give him the bad news. Dismounting the big sail, repairing it on a hot deck, and re-mounting the workhorse of a sail are going to be huge jobs.

When Bill wakes, I tell him about the sail. He looks, shrugs, and replies, "We'll fix it when the sun is not so intense." He lets the sail haul out without a worry that conditions will extend the rip.

Bill repairing sail with sail tape while underway.

Later in the afternoon when the sun is lower, Bill takes a lanyard from the cockpit railing and goes on deck to the furled genoa. He ties the line to the clew of the sail and the other end to the lifeline. I let the sail fly a bit so that the bottom is held parallel to the boat deck at about shoulder height. Bill applies a sail tape patch to the easily reached rip and then another to the reverse side of the sail. We watch the sail flutter in the breeze for signs of more needed patches. After a few minutes, he pronounces the repairs okay, removes the restraining line, and I ease the sheet to let the sail fly at its full normal set.

A major crisis for me is a minor bump to Bill.

James E. Keen

Day #23, Thursday, February 10, 2005
Noon Position: 15 deg. 26 min S, 6 deg. 58 min W
1,660 nautical miles to Fernando de Noronha
Noon-to-Noon Run: 118 nautical miles

❧   ❧   ❧

Bill's Email Dispatch

The Dell laptop computer connected to the SSB radio for sending and receiving email is mounted on a shelf over the chart table where it is protected from water. It is stuck to the shelf with Velcro to keep it from flying in rough conditions.

Jim's computer is newer and doesn't have a diskette drive, only a CD drive. To send anything he writes requires writing to a CD for import to the Dell. To swap CDs in the Dell disk drive, I have to pry the computer up from the sticky Velcro, bending it alarmingly, hold it in midair trying to wrench the old CD out, and balance everything while I put in the new CD. The process works but is tedious with normal boat motion.

❧   ❧   ❧

My midnight watch has good sailing on a black overcast night. During the next watch, Bill closes the boat as showers sweep in from directly astern. Later in the morning, the weather clears but the wind increases. We're boiling along now at six point five knots under genoa and trysail. It amazes me how quickly sailing conditions change.

I've developed a spreadsheet for displaying average daily speed and average trip speed. On the Simon's Town to Saint Helena leg, the fastest daily run averaged six point five knots on Day Three. We averaged four point seven knots for the entire trip. Day Nine was slowest at four point zero four knots. Since leaving Saint Helena we have averaged four point four two knots. The fastest twenty-four hour run was four point nine two knots on Day Two.

156

Day #24, Friday, February 11, 2005
Noon Position: 11 deg. 45 min S, 15 deg. 52 min W
1,091 nautical miles to Fernando de Noronha
Noon-to-Noon Run: 119 nautical miles

🪶 🪶 🪶

<u>Bill's Email Dispatch</u>

It's a clear day with blue sky and just a few puffy clouds. It has been overcast almost every day since Saint Helena, but last night the stars were out. This is trade wind sailing in the 5s, twin poles, very comfortable.

When we were on the tour of Saint Helena, at one point on the curvy lush mountain road, we passed a side trail going up Dana Mountain, marked Haley's Hill. A reader sent the following:

You might find it interesting that Saint Helena actually played a part in astronomers' quest to measure stellar distance. Edmond Haley in 1676 established an observatory on Diana's peak in order to measure the distance to both the Sun and Mercury. Observers in England and Europe were supposed to coordinate observation of Mercury when it was in opposition in 1677. Haley did his part, but only one astronomer back home did theirs so he could not do any meaningful calculation (cooperation between competing scholars was a problem even then). Good try but no horseshoe . . . but he was on the right track.

No, I'm not full of useless info. I just happen to be reading <u>Parallax;</u> <u>The Race to Measure the Cosmos</u>, by Alan Hirshfeld.

🪶 🪶 🪶

We raise the drifter early on this splendid day to try to maintain our excellent twenty-four hour progress. It is eighty-six degrees, more

157

humid, and small squalls catch up and pass regularly. We both feel rested, relaxed, and well-fed except for a craving for fruit. I'm hoarding the canned peaches and pineapple stash for later.

While Bill has the afternoon watch, I prepare scrambled eggs and Spam for lunch.

Later, on my double bunk, I lie under the open forward hatch to enjoy the windy backwash from the drifter and genoa. It is cool as I read and then snooze.

Today we've sailed 644 nautical miles on this leg and 2,354 nautical miles on the entire trip. That's almost half the expected 5,400 nautical mile trip.

Wow!

Trinidad Express

Day #25, Saturday, February 12, 2005
Noon Position: 10 deg. 55 min S, 17 deg. 46 min W
969 nautical miles to Fernando de Noronha
Noon-to-Noon Run: 122 nautical miles

❧ ❧ ❧

Bill's Email Dispatch

We have higher humidity, some showers around with broken clouds and an 85-degree temperature. At sunset, we take down the drifter and set the trysail. In the morning we take down the trysail and set the drifter. In between, we eat, sleep, and work on personal projects.

We are in the middle of the ocean, about 1,000 nautical miles from Africa and South America. We have stopped getting farther away from land and are now getting closer to land.

❧ ❧ ❧

As Advent II continues to sail well at four point five to six knots during my midnight watch, a woman broadcasts on the SSB from a nearby sailboat. She reports hearing an engine, going topside to see a large container ship too close for comfort. Wow, what a shock that must have been.

We've seen nothing manmade during the trip, except two ships early on. You'd expect to see some of the infamous plastic ocean trash that I hear infests the Atlantic, making it a cesspool. Where are the airplane contrails? We've seen absolutely nothing. Just a big, clean, sparkling pure ocean!

Day #26, Sunday, February 13, 2005
Noon Position: 10 deg. 11 min S, 19 deg. 35 min W
854 nautical miles to Fernando de Noronha
Noon-to-Noon Run: 115 nautical miles

🚩 🚩 🚩

<u>*Bill's Email Dispatch*</u>

Fifteen knots of wind from 115°, course 295°. Twin poles again on another beautiful day. We are sailing in the high 5s and low 6s but the motion is so gentle it doesn't feel that fast. The water speed indicator has stopped working, so I do not know how much of the boat speed is from the current.

We are now sailing with three other boats that left Saint Helena two days apart. One boat, Joy from Finland, is about 70 miles from us; a French boat, Tiki, and Espiritu from Denmark are about 200 miles away. Those three have sailed together and know each other. We are newcomers. At Saint Helena, nobody had dinghies in the water so that we could visit. The only time people really got together was aboard the water taxi, so we did not get to know them very well. Twice a day, they get together on the shortwave net to compare positions, weather, fishing, etc. I join in when I have something to contribute.

Behind us, another eight boats, the people we got to know around South Africa, are just arriving in Saint Helena. They also get together on the radio, and I have talked to some of them, but I guess we have sailed away and are no longer part of that group.

We will gather again in Trinidad.

🚩 🚩 🚩

I'm sitting in the cool cockpit during my midnight watch staring at the incredible waves and how Advent II and Windy handle them. I should,

160

by rights, be scared of some of the monster wave sequences, but I have faith in our trusty boat. She knows what to do, and gets it right every time.

When you look at the compass, you'll notice that Windy's steering course wanders this way and that. However, our sum-total course over time takes us efficiently on a nearly straight course to our destination.

Advent II is gyrating forty-five degrees from side to side and pitching up and down like a wild horse, making me hold on with white knuckles, glad to be wearing the inflatable life jacket and tether that securely fasten me to the boat.

A fiery trail illuminates the water in our turbulent wake, where tiny points of white light flash like sparklers. An occasional basketball-sized sphere lights up with phosphorescence. I am mesmerized by the brilliant display of glowing plankton.

The noise in the cockpit is constantly changing with the gurgle of water boiling past the stern, the swish-swish of waves sliding down the hull, the crash of a crest being caught under the platform at the stern, the report of a sail backwinded and recovering with a sharp crack, the muffled crash of white-caps in the dark, and the constant low background roar of the sea. As our speed increases, the noise becomes almost deafening.

* * * * * *

We sailed all night and morning at five point five to six point five knots using the wing-n-wing drifter and jib. The weather is getting hotter and more humid, uncomfortable in the cabin during the day. It's very unwise to stay in the cockpit during the hot part of the day because of sun glare and reflection. I keep a towel close for wiping sweat, but Bill seems to stay cool and comfortable.

Back on Saint Helena, we heard rumors that Mama Anne at Anne's Place made very good mashed potato fish cakes. We didn't get a chance to eat one. To vary the menu a bit last week, I decided to make my version. It was pretty bad. I failed to add eggs as a binder to the instant mashed potatoes. The result was a mushy, crumbly mess.

Today I get it right! I make eight golden brown mashed potato fish cakes served with whole kernel corn and big fat string beans. Nonetheless, I find using hot oil in an open frying pan on a gimbaled stove during rough weather a challenge.

Day #27, Monday, February 14, 2005
Noon Position: 9 deg. 14 min S, 21 deg. 17 min W
739 nautical miles to Fernando de Noronha
Noon-to-Noon Run: 115 nautical miles

❧   ❧   ❧

Bill's Email Dispatch

Wind 15 knots, twin poles, 100% overcast, and comfortable seas.

❧   ❧   ❧

We sail moderately three point five to five knots all night, and I wake to an overcast day with strengthening winds that blow hard in the patches of would-be storms. I say would-be because most of the disturbed clouds slide off with little effect. One squall did cause us to reef the drifter since we were seven knots. When going that fast, the likelihood of ripping the drifter is great. I lower and stow the sail for an hour, then raise it again to resume its work-horse spot beside the genoa. Bill sleeps right through this sail change and lets me do the trick on the pitching foredeck.

That was a new first. Bill seems to be more comfortable with my familiarity with the boat. There was never any question about my overall sailing ability. He just had to assure himself that I could be trusted to not fall off or put the boat in danger. Maybe I have passed the test.

We're beginning to think about Fernando and what we'll find in this nature preserve. The island is two hundred miles off the coast of Brazil at the extreme eastern bulge of South America. We've heard that when you tell the officials your next port is Trinidad, they wink and treat you differently. You're declared an unofficial stop which allows you to avoid visa, yellow fever, and malaria shot requirements. Officials just take our money for fees and do not stamp our passports.

163

Day #28, Tuesday, February 15, 2005
Noon Position: 8 deg. 34 min S, 22 deg. 59 min W
630 nautical miles to Fernando de Noronha
Noon-to-Noon Run: 109 nautical miles

✴ ✴ ✴

Bill's Email Dispatch

Wind southeast at 12 knots, seas smooth, twin poles, and boat speed in the high 4s. I think there are 16 different ways I can say that. I'll try not to use but six before we get to Noronha.

On this trip, I have had a new realization about provisioning. Not where and how, but what. We will find a market and buy fresh fruits and vegetables: apples, oranges, melons, plums, bananas, pineapple, mangoes, carrots, beans, cauliflower, onions, tomatoes . . . all that stuff. Then we start eating it. Some are cooked, some steamed, some raw. Some are consumed and some go bad and are tossed.

The mythology is that local is better than imported—and will keep longer. Pamplemousse, a French grapefruit from Polynesia, is one of those things; once you have eaten one you would gladly pay several times the cost of a regular grapefruit. But on the other hand, apples from Washington State are found around the world and are almost always better than local apples. I think the main reason local produce is so good is that it stays in the field until it is ripe. But that means that it will go bad sooner.

We have had some things that surprised us at how well they travel. Tomatoes have lasted for weeks. Honeydew melons seemed to never get old, only better. Some apples and some oranges last, some go bad. A bag of ripe, delicious oranges we bought in South Africa lasted until Saint Helena, and we still have some apples bought there. Only onions have always lasted until we ate all of them. Not so. A 100-pound bag of onions we got in Panama lasted until we had to surrender what we had

164

on board to the Australian health official months later. And they were really good onions.

The surprise has been carrots that go bad after only a few days. New Zealand carrots are larger, and better than any other carrots in the world, but will not keep a week. And here comes my new realization about provisioning. Before Jim arrived in South Africa, I bought a bag of carrots and those carrots are still good! The new realization is, buy whatever you want and whatever looks good. Some of it will go bad, but you will eat most of it. What you never know is what will go bad and what will last.

☀ ☀ ☀

The winds die on my midnight watch, so Bill starts the engine at 0400 hours when he comes on deck. I sleep past my usual wake up to come on deck at 0800 hours. The winds are still calm so I run the engine until about 1100 hours when I am able to raise the genoa and drifter, stow the trysail, and shut down the diesel. We've been moving well at four point five to five knots since.

James E. Keen

Day #29, Wednesday, February 16, 2005
Noon Position: 7 deg. 49 min S, 24 deg. 47 min W
515 nautical miles to Fernando de Noronha
Noon-to-Noon Run: 115 nautical miles

⚡ ⚡ ⚡

<u>*Bill's Email Dispatch*</u>

We have smooth seas, wind southeast at 12 knots, twin poles, boat speed in the high 4s.

A Typical Day:

A day for the Hebrews started at sundown. A day on the sailing ships of old went from noon to noon. (That is why a day's run on a boat is from noon to noon.) The celestial day starts when the sun crosses your meridian at noon, called a meridian transit. This is the one time when the ancient mariner sorta knew where they were. This is probably the reason the ship's day was from noon to noon.

For most people, the day starts when they get up in the morning, even though the civil day starts at midnight. My day starts when Jim strikes eight bells signaling first watch, from 2000 hours until 0000 hours. Sometimes I have dropped off into a deep sleep and sometimes I have just been dozing for the 45-minute nap. I get up, grab a cup of coffee, and relieve him on deck. He goes down, and I relish the time of coffee. Usually, it is two cups. I just sit in the dark cockpit, enjoying the waves, stars, the motion of the boat. I am alone, everything is fine, and God's creation is beautiful.

After about an hour, the second cup is empty and I will go below to use the computer. It is the best time for email propagation and I mess around with Winlink and Sailmail for a while, twiddling the shortwave radio and calling up various stations on the computer. I write short responses and send them. About 2300 hours propagation has died and

166

my brain is getting sleepy. I turn off all the lights and sit in the cockpit as the boat sails herself into the night.

At midnight I strike eight bells. It is Jim's watch until 0400 hours. Many times he is already awake and sometimes he relieves me a few minutes early. I crawl into the bunk. I sleep in the after cabin on the port side. I have boat cushions and soft side luggage arranged so the sleeping width is 22 inches wide, just the right width for me to wedge myself to resist the rolling of the boat. At 0400 hours Jim strikes eight bells.

I get up, grab a cup of coffee and relieve him on deck. He goes down and I relish the time of coffee. Usually, it is two cups. I just sit in the dark cockpit, enjoying the waves, stars, the motion of the boat. I am alone, everything is fine, and God's creation is beautiful.

After about an hour the second cup is empty and the eastern sky is getting light. Bucketing is accomplished in the cockpit unless we are in a closed harbor, in public, or in inclement conditions, when we use Virginia, the composting toilet.

My breakfast is usually oatmeal, but sometimes a leftover serving of last night's supper or a peanut butter and jam sandwich if we have bread. Jim is usually up between 0700 hours and 0800 hours. We talk, and change the sails from the night spread of trysail with poled genoa to poled drifter and poled genoa. I go back to bed for a nap, which lasts from two to five hours. I have never gotten so much sleep.

Sometime around noon, I will wake, usually well-rested. We will talk, cook, do some chores, and this is when I do most of my writing and try to catch up on correspondence. This is the time of hot sun and we both spend most of the time in the cabin, only going topside to answer the ten-minute timer.

We eat anytime between 1300 hours and 1700 hours, sometimes supper, sometimes a can of fruit, peaches or pineapple being favorites. As evening comes we will use the garden sprayer for a cockpit shower. It is amazing how refreshing that is. Then just before dark, we change

167

the sails back to trysail. nytime between 1800 hours and 1830 hours I will go down for a nap and my day has ended.

✼ ✼ ✼

Paradise just keeps getting better, day after day. When I come on deck, Bill is thinking about the usual daytime sail arrangement of wing-n-wing drifter and genoa. However, after looking at our five point five knot speed, he decides that we should leave the sails in the nighttime arrangement—wing-n-wing trysail and genoa.

Bill talked to Hans on Joy this morning and compared positions. Hans has five more miles to go on his GPS but is north and east of us. I've been looking for him all morning—no Joy. It's a really big ocean. Two other boats are ahead of us and plan to arrive tomorrow or Friday. We hope to arrive on Sunday.

After his morning nap, Bill gets out his bread making gear. We were really disappointed with the Saint Helena bread, reportedly the best in the world! It was bland with little taste and had a general hardness that was more than just a hard crust. The Simon's Town bread was far better, and Bill's bread is usually soft and fresh.

Trinidad Express

Day #30, Thursday, February 17, 2005
Noon Position: 6 deg. 50 min S, 26 deg. 37 min W
390 nautical miles to Fernando de Noronha
Noon-to-Noon Run: 125 nautical miles

❧ ❧ ❧

Bill's Email Dispatch

The wind has picked up to about 15 knots, and we are sailing wing-n-wing at a delightful 5+ knots. We should make landfall Monday, and at this rate, it may be before daylight. The boats we are sailing with will be already there and I can ask them over the radio about the harbor. It will be a full moon with an open ocean approach and shallow water a long way out, so if we get there at night we may be able to anchor well out away from any obstacles or other boats.

This little timer we are using has changed the way watches are kept, and I recommend it to anyone who needs to keep a lookout. It is about two inches wide, three inches long, and less than an inch thick. It lies flat so it does not tip over, has two small buttons, and one big button. We keep it in a zip-lock bag for protection and the plastic bag keeps it from sliding around. It is set for ten minutes and we keep it in the cockpit. It is loud enough to get your attention even if you are at the bow and the engine is running. Push the big button once to silence the alarm and again to restart the timer for another ten minutes. Look around, forget the timer, and go back to what you were doing. Ten minutes later you are again reminded to check the situation.

The timer lets you concentrate on what you are doing, reading, using the computer, doing maintenance, whatever and still not miss a situation check. An unexpected benefit is that, after living on a rigid ten-minute schedule for several weeks, my body clock is set for ten minutes. Jim and I will be in the cockpit talking and I will just automatically stand up to look around. Within seconds the timer will make its alarm sound. My body has anticipated the ten-minute time

169

lapse. Sometimes while groping in the dark the wrong button will get pushed and the alarm will not sound. But at almost exactly ten minutes, I will automatically look around, right on schedule.

When I am back in the U.S., I want to buy two more, just to make sure the first one will never stop working. It is called the Goodcook #33715 Timer by Bradshaw International, 800-421-6290.

✹ ✹ ✹

Trinidad Express

Day #31, Friday, February 18, 2005
Noon Position: 5 deg. 48 min S, 28 deg. 41 min W
253 nautical miles to Fernando de Noronha
Noon-to-Noon Run: 137 nautical miles

✦ ✦ ✦

Bill's Email Dispatch

We have been sailing at 6 knots for a full day now. Sailing at 5 knots for two days will get us there during the day Saturday.

This is the first ocean I have been in where there are almost no birds. Occasionally we will see a small black bird which I think is a petrel. There should be a reference book on ocean birds on board.

On the other hand, we have seen more fish than ever before. It is exciting to see fish swimming near the back of the boat.

The big deal last night was that we saw a ship, the first ship since the first day out of Cape Town. We are closing on continental South America and almost all shipping bound for the Panama Canal or the U.S. will converge as it rounds the eastern tip of Brazil, right where we are.

✦ ✦ ✦

In the last three days, we've had the wind from the best direction in the right strength. Thanks to this, each day resulted in great runs and we hardly touched the sails.

Shortly after midnight, a ship showing red running lights, a white bow light, and lots of lights on the big stern wheelhouse appears off the starboard stern. I knock on the deck to alert the sleeping Captain and turn on the radar to confirm the boat's track. It is going to pass easily off the starboard at a distance, according to the radar, of four miles. Bill

171

goes back to sleep, and I watch civilization for forty-five minutes as it fades into the forward horizon.

With the strong winds and high boat speed, it's hold-on time below. For the most part, I have learned to anticipate boat movements and hold on as she rolls from side to side. Miscalculating her movement spills me.

This morning in the cockpit with Bill, he asks me to tweak the lines on Windy. As I move aft on the starboard side, Advent II goes the other direction and I come down hard, catching the steel seat back on my left side kidney area. The pain is bearable but deep breathing and coughing hurts.

Bill doctors me with ibuprofen and I feel better. "Just wait until tomorrow. It will really hurt then!" he cautions.

Trinidad Express

Day #32, Saturday, February 19, 2005
Noon Position: 4 deg. 42 min S, 30 deg. 36 min W
123 nautical miles to Fernando de Noronha
Noon-to-Noon Run: 130 nautical miles

🚩   🚩   🚩

Bill's Email Dispatch

Air temperature is 89 degrees with water temperature of 82 degrees. After all, we are 282 nautical miles from the equator!

The earth is an approximate sphere. The equator is a circle of 360 degrees and each degree has 60 minutes of arc, not time. So there are 360 x 60 = 21,600 minutes of arc in a circle. It was decided that there would be that many nautical miles around the earth at the equator. So the circumference of the earth at the equator is 21,600 nautical miles.

At first, a nautical mile was 6,000 feet long. Then they recalculated the earth circumference and redefined a nautical mile as 6,080 feet long. They measured the earth again and the nautical mile changed again. Because the accuracy of the measurement or the size of the earth keeps changing they gave up on making it exactly one minute of arc. The nautical mile is now set at 6,076.11549 feet, approximately.

That makes our statute mile distance to Noronha to be: (6,076.11549 x 123) divided by 5,280 feet = 141.5458722 statute miles, approximately.

🚩   🚩   🚩

Doctor Bill is right. It does hurt more the next day. He prescribes acetaminophen, four times a day. I don't think I've broken a rib and do not have a fever. Maybe, I just have a bruise.

We have great winds all day and fly wing-n-wing drifter and genoa. In the afternoon, I lie on the double bunk under the open forward hatch,

173

daydreaming while looking at the sails and feeling the cooling wind of the sail backwash. I roll over to relieve the painful pressure on my side and look at my book without much enthusiasm.

"Wham!"

The sudden sound makes me jump. I look upward and see the drifter has a funny shape.

"Captain, we've got trouble!"

It takes only a few minutes to corral the wounded drifter and stuff it below. We free the trysail and boom it out wing-n-wing with little speed penalty.

Later, when we examine the drifter, the headboard has simply ripped from the sail. There was just too much force for the designed load of the thin light material. We'll stow the wounded sail until we get a chance to repair it in a calm anchorage on Noronha.

Day #33, Sunday, February 20, 2005
Noon Position: 3 deg. 47.05 min S, 32 deg. 15.8 min W
4 nautical miles to Fernando de Noronha
Noon-to-Noon Run: 126 nautical miles

Arrival day always changes things aboard. I am up at 0600 hours and we have an early lovely academic conversation about something as we normally do. Bill turns in a little early for his nap so he can be fresh for landfall. We only have a little over twenty miles to go, but we've not yet sighted the island.

We have no idea what to expect.

Just before 1000 hours, I see a ship several miles away coming from the north on what appears to be a collision course. Per standing orders, I go below, turn on the radar, and call the Captain.

While he is clearing sleep from his head, I hail the ship giving my position relative to his course. The ship answers saying he has us on radar and will pass close behind us. That seems ok to me, but it appears it is going to be a close encounter.

When Bill arrives on deck, he looks over the situation and says, "Jim, Rule Number One: Never pass in front of a ship!"

He calls the ship to request a port-to-port passage. I shift the genoa from starboard to port so we can turn ninety degrees to starboard. We sail north, passing port-to-port within a half-mile of the ship before turning again on our westward course.

A lesson well learned for me, one that puts me in charge instead of some unknown radar operator on a ship.

The rule: if you can see the ship, it is too close to cross its bow!

"Land Ho!"

Bill had just settled again in the cabin when the island appears in the distant haze. We'd earlier discussed that the impending landfall could not possibly rival the beauty of the Saint Helena landfall. We were right; the Fernando landfall is not quite up to that level. But, lofty volcanic peaks appear to rise from the sea exactly where the GPS has predicted after three thousand miles of travel from South Africa.

The landfall does make a great entrance to the South American continent.

Chapter 5

Fernando de Noronha: Ecotourism in the Tropics

Fernando de Noronha is a cluster of islands located two hundred twenty miles off the eastern Brazilian coast. Often called the Brazilian Galapagos, the islands are known for ecological tourism and recreational SCUBA diving.

The archipelago is a UNESCO World Heritage Site, one of 936 worldwide sites listed in 2011. Because of the area's importance as a feeding ground for several marine species, a high population of dolphins, and the preservation of endangered species, it has earned this designation among eighteen such sites in Brazil.

Of the twenty-one islands of Fernando de Noronha, only the largest is inhabited. Rich island coastal waters are important for the breeding and feeding of tuna, shark, turtle, and marine mammals. Baia de Golfinhos has an exceptional population of dolphin while the Rocas Atoll provides tidal pools teeming with fish. Noronha supports the largest concentration of tropical seabirds in the Western Atlantic.

A submerged range of volcanic mountains forms the base of the islands, rocks, and islets that make the archipelago. The main island is six point two miles by two point one seven miles with an area of seven point one square miles. The ocean floor is 2,480 feet below the sea surface.

The main island of Fernando de Noronha makes up 91% of the land area with the remainder in small islands and islets. The upland central plain of Fernando is known as the Quixaba.

The Rocas Atoll, Saint Peter and Paul Rocks, and the volcanic spire on the Beach at Conceicao are some of the spectacular sites in the area.

There is a rainy season from March to September with little rainfall for the rest of the year.

The island was discovered by Amerigo Vespucci in 1503. Fernando de Noronha was given by the Florentine Crown to a Portuguese lord, Fernão de Loronha, from whom it takes its name. After periods of occupation by the English, Dutch, and French, Portugal decided to fortify the main island by building ten stone forts.

Traditional boats and a new windmill show island contrasts.

In the 19th century, the island was a penal colony and the extensive native forests were cleared to prevent prisoners from building wooden escape boats. As a consequence, today's rocky and barren landscape has only scattered pockets of stunted trees. Noronha was later used to isolate political prisoners and became a Federal Territory in 1942.

During World War II, Brazilian political dissidents were housed in a prison on the island. During that same period, the U.S. Army Air Force Air Transport Command built an airport to provide a transoceanic air route between Brazil and French West Africa.

In 1988, the islands became a District of the State of Pernambuco, Brazil. The Governor appoints an island manager for the increasingly popular tourist attraction.

Today, the island is a popular eco-tourist destination.

James E. Keen

Our Island Visit

At noon, we are only four miles from our Fernando de Noronha, Brazil waypoint, but it takes two hours to sail around the northern coastline to a small open ocean roadstead. A volcanic spire towers over the harbor while large volcanic rocks seem to have been flung about at random. An L-shaped breakwater protects a tiny refuge harbor against the ocean swell that crashes violently ashore. A popular sandy bathing beach is in the protected area.

We motor among the twelve visiting yachts before selecting a spot and dropping anchor near Joy, Espiritu, and Tiki, our traveling friends. It's a weird experience to see neighboring boats downhill, and then a

Harbor Scene at Fernando de Noronha, Brazil with colorful local boats and a volcanic piton in the background.

few seconds later, uphill from you as the long smooth swell raise, and then lower, the sea level in passing.

We snub the anchor, stow seagoing deck gear, and unlash the dinghy parts from the portside lifeline. After carrying the components onto the less-cluttered foredeck, we unfold sides and bottom, insert and bolt the transom and three seats that double as stiffeners, and then add the outboard engine. A jib halyard lifts the dinghy and deposits it into the sea. Shirley is overboard for the first time since the Indian Ocean.

Bill in Port-A-Boat Shirley with cruise boat in background.

A Venezuelan cruise ship has anchored a half mile off our stern, and boats flit about ferrying cruise passengers ashore. Local boats, that provide ecological and SCUBA outings, produce a constant churn and clog the tiny protected dock area with confused seas.

James E. Keen

Towering over this windy scene, dwarfed by the nearly one thousand foot volcanic finger-like Pico Mountain, is the island power source: a tall, slender, white steel tube, topped with a modern electric power generating windmill. It's a recent addition to augment the island diesel generator.

We talk on the VHF to Hans on Joy about island entry procedures. He says we should go ashore soon to see the Port Captain. He's located at the top of the jetty.

Shirley slides onto the sandy beach and we thread our way through Sunday afternoon sunbathers. The Harbor Master's office is at the end of the rock jetty at the parking area.

We have a bit of a communications problem, as islanders speak Portuguese and we speak eastern North Carolina-accented English. Port Captain Antonio uses grunts and gestures to help us complete formal procedures. As we had already heard, we do not officially enter Brazil, and do not receive a passport stamp. Antonio, however, uses his Visa machine to get his US$250 for our three-day stay.

He gestures a stern warning to strictly obey the Natural Preserve rules. The entire island coastline is a wildlife preserve. SCUBA diving and Ecological Tourism is big business, so he is happy to give us a brochure that is printed in English.

It's Sunday and most island businesses are closed but we want beer and fruit. We have no Real (Brazilian money), so we can't catch the bus or taxi. Not knowing what to do, we flirt with several local teenage girl Greeters that have gathered to assist cruise ship passengers. One helpful English-speaking beauty leads us across the port parking area to an open-air health food stand. She arranges an exchange of US$20 for R$48.

The stand is nothing more than four brick columns holding up a substantial orange tile roof. A bar occupies one end with serving tables scattered about the other end. We sit at the bar, buy two beers, and share a toast of our successful crossing of the Southern Atlantic Ocean.

An attractive lady from the cruise ship sits on the next barstool and engages us in English with a pleasant Venezuelan accent. She is a cruise ship social director and has escaped her hectic life for a few hours ashore. After talking about our crossing, she tells us about Noronha.

Brazil's EPA, Ibama, strictly limits private businesses on the island. Closely supervised tourism is the major source of island jobs with most of the three thousand permanent residents working in the one hundred or so small pousadas (bed and breakfast) and restaurants that are sprinkled along the twenty-three sparkling beaches. Visitors, strictly limited to four hundred twenty at a time, are required to pay a tax to support ecological preservation and to finance mundane tasks like carting all sewage to the mainland for processing.

Fernando de Noronha Airport has several daily flights from Recife and Natal on the Brazilian coast bringing tourist to the island. Cruise ships make the islands a port of call but must anchor offshore and ferry passengers to the single dock.

The Real (plural Reais) is the Brazilian currency with a 2005 value of about R$2.40 for each U.S. dollar. In 2010, Noronha had a per capita income of R$10,001.

During that same year, the island played a major role in the search for, and the eventual recovery, of the downed French airliner. The crash site is hundreds of miles away in the Atlantic north of Noronha, but the airport is the closest facility for search and rescue aircraft.

Our attractive information source decides it is time to catch a taxi to see inland friends. We say goodbye and drink two more beers, then eat a refreshing grape ice cream dish topped with granola, bananas, and Mango slices. I decide health food with beer is not bad when you consider our Spartan meals for the past month.

We make phone calls to our wives, catching up on hometown news in somewhat lengthy international collect calls. While drinking another beer, we watch the cruise ship turn on lights to become a lighted jewel among deepening shadows against a spectacular orange sunset.

Shirley renegotiates the swell to take us to Advent II. At 2100 hours, we crash for the night. Exploring Fernando de Noronha will keep until tomorrow.

Day #34, Monday, February 21, 2005
Fernando de Noronha

Relaxation and Wild Dune Buggy Rides

The second day after arrival is often a lazy one. The first day ashore is spent getting to know something about the area and celebrating with a few congratulatory drinks. The second day is for recuperating. We sleep

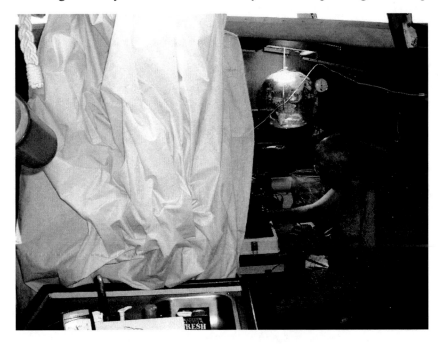

Bill repairing sails at the salon table.

late, wash clothes in the cockpit, and putter around the boat until late afternoon. I spend too long in the midday sun tending to my drying clothes and despite using my SPF 50, hat, and good sunglasses, I feel a bit touchy from face and neck sunburn for a few days. You'd think that

185

I would have learned to avoid the sun during the middle of the day since I have been doing just that for the past thirty-three days.

Bill spends much of the morning repairing the genoa and drifter. He sets up his industrial quality sewing machine on the main salon table. I feed the large sails down the main hatch for repair as he remakes the headboard of the drifter and stitches over worn seams on the genoa. He does the same for the rest of the sail inventory. Not only are the seams worn and unraveling, the Dacron fabric is stiff with UV damage from sun exposure. The sails are just tired, as they should be, nearing the completion of a world circumnavigation.

Police Dune Buggy at Fernando de Noronha, Brazil

Monday also brings the exodus of the cruising fleet. Of the thirteen cruising sailboats in the harbor on Sunday, all but six leave this morning. Espiritu, Tiki, and Joy are set to leave on Tuesday, and that will leave only the Brazilian yacht, a small locally owned sailboat at the far side of the harbor, and Advent II.

* * * * * *

Things are still buzzing in the port with cruise ship passengers and resort guests milling about. Locals scramble to accommodate their guests with marine outings. We need local cash to buy fuel so we look for a ride to the airport where the only island ATM machine is located.

Cars are scarce—the Port Captain has one—but trucks are numerous. Everything is imported from the mainland by boat and distributed about the island by truck. Buses are common on the public bus routes, and more upscale buses are used to ferry the resort guests about.

Our dune buggy taxi with Jim riding on the rear.

Then there's the ubiquitous dune buggy. Young people and the police drive classic dune buggies, equipped with air-cooled Volkswagen engines with that unforgettable whining sound. Our taxi is a dune buggy. Bill has long legs, so he gets to sit up front. I sit high on the elevated padded rear deck with white knuckles clutching the roll bar as we roar off, leaving a cloud of blue exhaust smoke. I hold on tightly as we negotiate the curvy one-lane-plus road to the airport.

Fernando de Noronha Airport is small but modern, and we easily locate the Reais dispensing ATM. On the return trip, we putt-putt our way past well-hidden, modest, and sturdy stucco homes, where locals live effectively separated from tourists staying in lavish villas.

James E. Keen

With local cash in hand, we go to the supermarket.

I was suckered by the taxi driver, paying R$20 fare each way per person, or R$40 total, about US$18. Later we find that we could have ridden the bus for R$2.50 each way. Since I have paid so well for the ride, the taxi driver shows us around a less than stellar market. Perhaps the market belongs to a relative, or maybe it is an attempt to support the local owner, rather than a much nicer foreign chain grocery next door.

We buy little in this local market and Bill goes over to the chain market while I visit the bakery and a produce vendor under a nearby shade tree. With two big cloth bags full of fresh produce and other groceries, we hop back into the dune buggy and return to the port.

We visit the Health Food Bar for dinner of Ashi (Amazonian fruit) ice cream topped with granola, bananas, and honey and served with a side of beer. The cruise ship departs and within an hour, the port is almost deserted.

Shirley deposits us home after plowing through some rather large swells. We spend the remainder of the evening preparing for departure.

Day #35, Tuesday, February 22, 2005
Fernando de Noronha

Water and Fuel Replenishment

Bill determines that water should be my priority. I take Shirley to the dock to see the Port Captain about obtaining potable water. A policeman tells me the Port Captain would not arrive until maybe 0800 or 0830 hours.

He bombards me with a volley of questions, not official, but about the English language. He writes excellent English, but his speaking and syntax are weird. I spend the hour tutoring his English.

"Is it make you out?" he asks.

"No, it's make out!" I reply.

He peppers me with similar questions of other such nonsense. His very serious questions give some idea of what an island of beautiful young people mixed with mainland tourists can be like.

Port Captain Antonio arrives. When I ask about the absence of potable water at the port, he appears very embarrassed. Their potable water system is broken but he charged us full price that should have included potable water.

"I can't help it," is his halting gesture. "You'll have to buy water, in twenty-liter bottles, at the market."

Antonio does, however, offer his car and driver to accomplish my task. I thank him and tell him I need to make a quick trip back to the boat for my Visa card.

* * * * * *

189

My ride is a shiny new official red Toyota sedan. At the market, the driver helps me empty the large twenty-liter bottles into our four twenty-four-liter deck jugs. I then buy five more bottles for a total of eleven, about fifty gallons. We load them into the trunk of the car.

We find Port Captain Antonio at the harbor watching a crew unload bricks, by hand, from a small wooden coastal freighter. I watch as laborers in a long line toss bricks down from the boat and along the line to be stacked on the truck. Limited by the small dockage facilities, all supplies arrive from the mainland in small boats and are unloaded in this crude manner.

Antonio and the driver help me haul the heavy water jugs down concrete steps to Shirley tied alongside the slippery seaweed-covered rocks. I take my digital camera from its waterproof zip-lock baggie and snap photos of the smiling men. I put the camera in my pants pocket, then turn to board Shirley. I slip on the rocks and take an unexpected head first seawater dunk. Scrambling back onto the rocks, I find that I'm all in one piece but my camera, out of its protective bag, is ruined. My wallet is soaked and the handheld VHF radio is wet but is splash proof and dries without harm. Sadly, I probably lost all the pictures I have taken since I last downloaded to my laptop.

I start the engine and in sopping wet clothes steer an overloaded Shirley around the end of the protective jetty. With very low freeboard, hauling four hundred pounds of water and my soggy two hundred seventy-five pound frame, I cautiously negotiate the choppy quarter-mile open ocean commute and arrive safely at Advent II.

As I tie up, I note from a prominent nameplate on the dinghy that the load limit is four-hundred-eighty pounds.

What a great boat!

* * * * * *

By late morning, I have the water jugs on board, individually chlorinated, and added to the main tanks. This was accomplished via Bill's precise way of dosing the water in each jug with chlorine rather

190

than dumping a large amount of chlorine into the main tank. Either method will accomplish the task, however, Bill insists on dosing each jug as a more precise method.

You'd think the water would taste bad after such treatment—but it's palatable. I've consumed at least two 2-liter bottles of treated water each day while at sea in the last month. I like it!

* * * * * *

We go ashore with fuel jugs and buy diesel fuel from a service station across the street from the harbor. It takes several dinghy trips to ferry fuel to the boat.

With water and fuel replenishment completed, we can relax and enjoy the island for another day and maybe have a caipirinha, Brazil's national drink. It's a cool brew of cachaça sugar cane rum, sugar, and lime.

"It's a big relief to get that done, Jim," Bill comments. "Maybe we can leave tonight!"

It is obvious that Bill is still worrying about standing up Grayson. Our Fernando de Noronha visit will not be a sightseeing stop.

Remember, this is The Trinidad Express.

* * * * * *

When I fell and hurt myself four days earlier, I was also suffering from constipation. The injury is healing rather well. It no longer hurts to cough, and I have twice muscled over four hundred pounds of water today without too much pain. However, I am now suffering my sixth day of constipation.

Bill puts on his EMT hat and says, "I'm not leaving until you have a complete evaluation. We're going to the hospital."

We don't know how to find the hospital, so we hire a dune buggy taxi.

James E. Keen

* * * * * *

The new, but deserted-looking, hospital building is on a hillside off the main road. We roar up an alleyway to the rear emergency entrance where we dismiss the rumbling bug taxi.

The Brazilian doctor is young, probably a resident, and speaks excellent English. He listens to my concerns of a possible injury caused blockage. He prescribes a powerful laxative, and says, "Come back tomorrow if it doesn't work."

I introduce Bill and tell the doctor of Bill's volunteer job as an emergency medical technician and his interest in medicine. The doctor spends a few minutes showing Bill the hospital's shiny equipment.

I ask about payment.

"Our care is free," the doctor says. "Our population is young and healthy, so our hospital is largely empty."

I insist on paying something. He suggests that I make a contribution to the hospital charity.

"You can't miss the pharmacy. It's just at the next square," the doctor says as we depart.

* * * * * *

In the commercial square about half a mile away, we can't find a pharmacy. A lounging young man offers to lead us there.

We retrace our steps on the main road and turn onto a scrawny woodland path to arrive at a small mixed residential and business area. At a nicely landscaped public area, a man is sweeping the street near an ancient cannon display next to a children's play area.

The pharmacy is a recycled shotgun house, much like we have in places in the U.S. A convenience store area with a snack bar occupies the front, while shelves of gifts, a small supply of medical remedies, and the pharmacy window occupy the rear.

192

My prescription is quickly filled.

I buy a new hat to replace the floppy beanie hat I left behind on an earlier bus ride. We buy postcards, orange drinks, and a beer and meat pie for our guide.

A bus arrives and the driver hands my beanie to me when we board. We roar off towards the port.

My wife will enjoy the blue Fernando de Noronha hat.

Day #36, Wednesday, February 23, 2005
Fernando de Noronha

✐ ✐ ✐

Bill's Email Dispatch

We departed Fernando de Noronha at 1000 hours on Wednesday 23 February, 2005, destination—Trinidad, distance, 1,828 nautical miles. We will be paralleling the South America coast, several hundred miles offshore.

✐ ✐ ✐

I spend a miserable night tossing about, getting up several times to attempt to move my bowels. When Bill and I share the cockpit for 0600 hours breakfast, I indicate my failure.

Bill considers this a moment, then replies, "We'll go get more water and fuel and see the doctor again."

By 0800 hours, we have most of the deck work complete and I have partially conquered my constipation. After a few more heroic attempts, I am mostly relieved, so the Captain announces, "Let's get underway!"

I winch in the anchoring gear, and at 1000 hours, the anchor is lashed on deck.

We get underway and the young folks on the Brazilian yacht wave while we motor out to sea.

We have spent three days at Fernando de Noronha instead of the scheduled five. We've made up two more days toward getting back to the original arrival date. At noon we are fifteen miles off the coast.

Fernando de Noronha is fading into the mist and our memories.

Chapter 6

Third Leg: Sailing to Trinidad

 Day #37, Thursday, February 24, 2005
Noon Position: 2 deg. 56 min S, 34 deg. 19 min W
1,828 nautical miles to Trinidad
Noon-to-Noon Run: 115 nautical miles

☙ ☙ ☙

Bill's Email Dispatch

So far, all the way from South Africa, the winds have been from the southeast. We are sailing northwest. Not once has the wind been forward of the beam. It's been poles all the way, classic trade wind sailing. The planning for the entire circumnavigation has been: trade wind sailing, and the avoidance of storms.

In the northern hemisphere the trade winds are northeast—no longer behind us but on our starboard beam.

But, we must get from here to there, crossing the doldrums, more commonly called the Inter Tropical Convergence Zone or ITCZ. Between the southeast trade winds and the northeast trade winds, along *the equator is this area of unstable weather with variable light winds, periods of calm, frequent showers and occasional severe squalls.*

Yesterday we noticed the weather change. It is hot, 87 degrees, and humid. The wind seems to vary between 5 and 10 knots and the boat speed from 3 to 5 knots. We had two rain showers last night and two today. This weather pattern will persist until the wind dies completely. The plan: motor directly to the north to get through the ITCZ. However, we'll have some frustrating days in between.

🗲 🗲 🗲

The Islands of Fernando de Noronha are splendid in their breathtaking beauty. We'll remember the rugged volcanic spires; the nature preserve; the friendly, healthy, beautiful native people; cruise ship tourists; resort tourists; and too many hard bodies hanging onto speeding, noisy dune buggies. We'll cherish the memory and hope my pictures survive the seawater dunking.

When we sailed from Fernando de Noronha yesterday, Bill's mental attitude changed completely. I saw the cares of shore side life melt away as he again engaged in his passion—practicing the art of sailcraft on Advent II.

He has his own unique way of doing things, and he can tell you his exact reasoning. He doesn't tell you that your way is wrong. Bill just says, "I do it this way because . . ." His conviction and logic win.

We do it Bill's way.

As the shoreline fades into the mist, we resume our offshore routine and Bill is in his element. I feel confident and ready for the last offshore hop.

* * * * * *

We had a good sail yesterday afternoon, but just before my midnight watch, Bill starts the engine. I let it run during my watch, and Bill finds enough wind on his watch to turn it off at 0500 hours. We set the drifter and fly our workhorse wing-n-wing sail plan with poled genoa and drifter.

After his morning nap, Bill decides to vacuum the boat.

"I always do it when the batteries are fully charged," he offers, justifying his actions.

He spends the next 30 minutes lifting floor hatches and vacuuming accumulated dirt from the bilge. This must be his version of spring cleaning—his South Atlantic cleaning.

At noon, I call Bill on deck to discuss a cloud approaching from the stern. It looks somewhat threatening, and I suggest we leave the drifter in place. Earlier, we had spent an hour on deck in the hot sun furling and redeploying the genoa, changing poles, and rigging the drifter.

Bill's rule: "If you think you should drop the sail, then don't delay, do it now!"

I scamper forward to lower the drifter while Bill puts on his deck gear. Everything goes wrong: the drifter halyard snags on the cleat at the base of the mast, snags again on my harness strap, and finally snags at the spreaders. In each case, I am ten feet or more from the snag while holding on to a wildly bouncing boat. Using a little teamwork, we clear the snags and I finally drop the wildly flogging sail.

As I tie the drifter to the lifeline, winds and rains come, whipped to a vengeful intensity. We've not seen rain this hard at any other time, but fortunately, it finishes and the sun is shining within minutes.

As we gather in the cockpit to dry off, we agree that Advent II is finally clean of all the accumulated salt of the Indian Ocean. The South Atlantic cleaning is complete.

* * * * * *

197

James E. Keen

I have suggested several times that Bill should cut my somewhat long hair. We have never gotten around to it. Out of the blue, Bill says, "Why don't we cut your hair?"

Bill gets out his battery-powered clippers and gives me the choice of an eighth-inch or quarter-inch guards. I sit on the coachroof as my golden-white locks fall to the deck and blow overboard. I go below and apply the clippers to my beard using Normandie's broken mirror.

I try to imagine why Bill had the thought to cut my hair. Is he just tired of looking at me with sweat-drenched hair? Or, maybe he feels that it's time that I looked less green! There are two Bill look-alike souls aboard now: both with white, short-cropped hair on a balding head and close-cropped white beard. I am the short fat one.

After the haircut, I find time to examine my soaked digital camera. It's had time to dry, so I replace the batteries and turn it on. It works—except the focus motor. Unfortunately, without a working focus, the images will be all fuzzy. The camera is useless but I am able to extract the SD card and download my digital pictures before I condemn it to the trash. Bill says he will share his camera for the rest of the trip.

* * * * * *

Bill spends time today trying to calculate when we'll make landfall at Trinidad. By applying the one-hundred-miles-per-day rule, we should arrive on March fifteenth. That's actually ahead of the original ETA of March nineteenth. Time remaining on this trip is getting short, but Bill is really paranoid about not leaving Grayson alone at the altar. It's time to start thinking about asking our wives to buy airplane tickets for a flight home.

In the meantime, I'll finish writing my log, have a luxurious cockpit shower, put on less-wet clothes, have a peaches and bananas dinner conversation in the cockpit, and start my midnight watch.

Sailcraft is so enjoyable!

Day #38, Friday, February 25, 2005
Noon Position: 1 deg. 55 min S, 35 deg. 47 min W
1,722 nautical miles to Trinidad
Noon-to-Noon Run: 106 nautical miles

❧ ❧ ❧

Bill's Email Dispatch

ITCZ—The southeasterly trades in the southern hemisphere and the northeasterly northern hemisphere trades flow together, and the air goes up. The warm humid air cools and forms huge rain clouds. Sploosh! It rains. Then the opposing winds cancel each other and the wind dies.

(1330 hours) It's hot, 89 degrees, very humid, and uncomfortable in the cabin during passing showers. Total overcast with ugly clouds. We were sailing on a course of 300° at less than 4 knots so I started the engine and came to a course of 330°. There is still enough wind to fill the sails. The speed is about 5.5 knots.

(1430 hours) Clear sky where we are. Big ugly cloud up ahead.

(1500 hours) Clear, beautiful blue sky. Some clouds on the horizon. Wind from the northeast. That is curious. Could it be that we have already passed through?

(1600 hours) 100% cloud cover. Still northeast wind.

(1700 hours) Sky has cleared. There is some dirty stuff behind us but all around there are nothing but white puffy clouds. The grib files show the ITCZ south of us and Trudy says the ITCZ is south of us. The Tropical Prediction Center in Miami also agrees, as does Ralph on Arjumand.

As I was writing, a shower came up and I had to go up and tail the winch while Jim furled the genoa.

199

Anyway, Arjumand is about 100 nautical miles ahead of us and they say that the wind is steady from the northeast and the bad stuff is over.

(1715 hours) Jim just pointed out a waterspout in a cloud ahead of us. This is no place to get complacent.

🌀   🌀   🌀

It is a slow messy night with the winds "blowing and slowing" as Bill says. On the morning Barbados Radio Net, we learn that the ITCZ is located just south of the equator, about two degrees. That's right where we are. Two degrees, or one hundred twenty miles, is just over a day's run so it looks like we'll sleep on top of a noisy diesel tonight.

Bill starts the diesel at 0800 hours. I trim the sails while hoping to get enough speed so we can shut off that blasted noisy thing.

At 1100 hours, after a series of strong squalls, the temperature drops noticeably and the wind veers into the east. We take in the portside pole and set the genoa without the pole in an ordinary day sailing fashion.

For the first time in more than a year, Advent II is on a reach, sailing with the wind from the side, rather than on the coconut milk run— sailing the trades with the wind always astern.

Bill says, "It'll take some getting used to down below. Everything changes on a starboard tack."

He is referring to the fact that for most of the circumnavigation, the wind has come from astern but now we have wind coming from abeam. How you walk, how you hold on, and how you negotiate the slanted sole and furniture below, changes when you change tack. All our muscle memory has to be relearned to accommodate the new slanted layout below.

* * * * * *

During our morning academic cockpit conversation, we discuss what we will do first at landfall in Trinidad. Bill chooses ice cream while I choose an endless hot shower.

This is Friday, but all the clothes I washed on Monday are either wet or smelly from not being dry enough before stowing.

That smell reminds me of my high school football career. I would wear a t-shirt under my football pads. After practice, I'd take off the t-shirt, put it in the locker, and then use the same stiff, smelly t-shirt the next day.

It's the same here. Put the stiff smelly t-shirt under the inflatable vest and harness, day after day.

Anyway, having an endless hot shower will be wonderful!

Day #39, Saturday, February 26, 2005
Noon Position: 0 deg. 20 min S, 65 deg. 49 min W
1,624 nautical miles to Trinidad
Noon-to-Noon Run: 98 nautical miles

✹   ✹   ✹

Bill's Email Dispatch

Overcast, misty rain that keeps everything wet but is not enough to collect for washing. The Wind is up and down from this way and that.

There are occasional passing showers with some moderate wind in very choppy seas. It's hot in the closed cabin and generally uncomfortable. So far we have had neither really heavy rain nor strong wind.

✹   ✹   ✹

"Ladies and gentlemen, we're speaking to you tonight from the verandah (cockpit) of the beautiful Sailing Vessel Advent II. We're sailing (actually motoring) over placid seas (actually semi-rough seas) on our approach to the equator. It's a balmy evening (actually a very humid eighty-eight degrees) under a full moon (actually hidden behind rain clouds) with a tropical shower in progress (repeated intense rain squalls all day). I hope you have enjoyed tonight's broadcast."

So went my watch dreams last night of old radio broadcasts from the ballroom of the Astoria in the heart of New York City. Clearly, I've been out here too long!

* * * * * *

Our short encounter with the ITCZ has now turned into a long encounter, and it's not over. We have motored since 1330 hours yesterday, through rain showers all night and all morning. When Bill takes the morning watch, I prepare a one-pot lunch. At 1430 hours,

202

during a heavy rain squall, we fill our plate and sit below, on the sole, while bracing as best we can to enjoy our meal. It is too rough and wet to eat in our luxurious dining cockpit.

The inside of our cabin is like a roller coaster or a carnival pirate ship rocking wildly back and forth. We hold on to safety hard points while the whole boats lurches forty-five degrees each way and slams into waves with a mighty crash that shakes everything. We race to get across the equator.

Surely, it will get better then.

* * * * * *

Bill sticks his head inside the main hatch and announces, "Two and a half miles to go!" He's been keeping a close watch on the GPS to capture photographic proof of our equator crossing moment. He has another picture from when he and Normandie crossed the equator into the southern hemisphere early in the voyage.

Mariners have always cheered the crossing of the equator with celebrations by shellbacks (multiple crossers) at the expense of pollywogs (first-time crossers). Since Bill is a shellback and I'm a pollywog, I'm anticipating the crossing with trepidation.

One tradition is to toast the god of the sea, Neptune, with a hearty belt of your dearest drink aboard. I wonder if Bill will lighten his ban on alcohol at sea for this momentous occasion.

No, way! Instead, he just pours a bit of our best rum, coffee, and Castle beer into the sea as a gesture to Neptune. I hope the god was not pissed. Bill took pictures and was nice to the pollywog. We were just too hot and wet for any shenanigans.

To get digital pictures of the GPS showing the latitude of all zeros at the equator, Bill turns the boat and runs straight down the line. His multiple shots of the GPS with the zero latitude should certainly capture the event.

Day #40, Sunday, February 27, 2005
Noon Position: 0 deg. 52 min N, 38 deg. 13 min W
1,519 nautical miles to Trinidad
Noon-to-Noon Run: 105 nautical miles

✺   ✺   ✺

Bill's Email Dispatch

We crossed the equator back into the northern hemisphere at 1705 hours yesterday.

Of course, we saluted Neptune with the proper oblations. He was pissed by our inept showing of respect and wrought havoc on us with eight hours of fierce, constantly changing wind and rain. We spent much of the time below in the steamy cabin until Neptune laughed and calmed down. Next time, it'll be whiskey for all hands and many salutes to Neptune.

So far we have not found one leak, so there is no accumulation of water and real dampness inside the boat that can make life miserable. And also so far we have had no wind in the showers to cause us real problems.

Sooner or later we will sail out of this mess.

✺   ✺   ✺

Trinidad Express

 Day #41, Monday, February 28, 2005
Noon Position: 1 deg. 54 min N, 39 deg. 55 min W
1,400 nautical miles to Trinidad
Noon-to-Noon Run: 119 nautical miles in 25 hours

🌀 🌀 🌀

<u>*Bill's Email Dispatch*</u>

The weather cleared yesterday afternoon, but the rains came again. There were showers after showers from about midnight until I went down for sleep at 0800 hours. Before the mist of one stopped, another was starting. We even got some substantial rainfall from some of them.

The wind has been coming and going, from this way and that. Sailing like that is tiring. I handed a soggy, slow boat over to Jim and went down.

Four hours later: I am refreshed, Jim is smiling, the sun is out, and we are on a beam reach going 6.6 knots!

"Have been since 0900 hours," Jim says.

Now this is traveling. Of course, we hope that this is what we will get out of the trade winds. It would be really good to do a few days at 6 knots.

The flogging has stopped, and morale has improved.

🌀 🌀 🌀

Heavy rain squalls blow past all night as the prevailing wind dies. Bill starts the diesel at 0400 hours and runs through the heavy rain until 0800 hours when he shuts off the noisy beast and retires for a peaceful and quiet sleep.

I go on deck and trim sails to increase our speed between the blasts of wind and calms that accompany rain showers. The flogging of the sails stops, and before long we are bounding along at six point six knots on a broad reach.

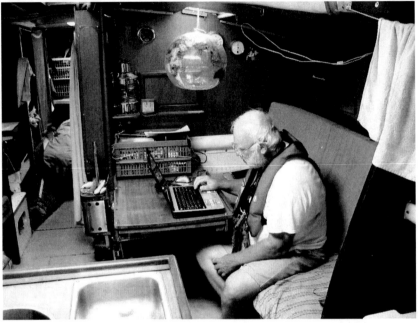

Jim using his laptop at salon table. Note his long hair, world globe and safety gear.

My spreadsheet indicates we have traveled 4,000 nautical miles from South Africa and we have 1,400 nautical miles to go to Trinidad.

* * * * * *

Today is sandwich day. The Fernando bread is going bad, the lush carrots are rotten, and the four South Africa eggs are suspect. When I use a SA egg, it erupts into a slimy orange mess. I throw the other three overboard. To use our remaining Saint Helena eggs, I think about serving fish cakes or pancakes but rule out that folly since it's too risky to cook with hot oil. So, it's sandwich and hold on time!

Bill declares another twenty-five hour day and changes our clocks to put us only two hours behind Eastern Standard Time.

Day #42, Tuesday, March 1, 2005
Noon Position: 3 deg. 06 min N, 42 deg. 8 min W
1250 nautical miles to Trinidad
Noon-to-Noon Run: 150 nautical miles

☙ ☙ ☙

<u>*Bill's Email Dispatch*</u>

That was a great 150-nautical-mile day! The northeast trades are steady and we are making excellent progress. It's SSS or Simply Superb Sailing.

Last night I saw lights on the horizon, turned on the radar per standing orders, and saw nothing. The lights came a little closer. Then on the VHF there was a call, "Vessel sailing westward at 6 knots. This is Sea Eagle." I answered, and he requested a one-whistle pass, port-to-port. When we were clear of each other, he informed me that he is a 660-foot tanker carrying vegetable oil from Cape Town to China. I asked how he first saw us, visual or radar. He said he picked us up visually at eight miles. I could hardly see his lights at eight miles, and he saw our single green running light. That's twice as far as my most optimistic hopes for our Aqua Signal series 40 running lights.

☙ ☙ ☙

We just completed one of the fastest daily runs ever for Advent II. She sails well on the Advent II Reach & Run. For you land lubbers, sailboats sail two ways: a reach, where the wind is forward or abeam of the mast; and a run, where the wind is aft of the mast. A reach requires the sails to be set up so that an aerodynamic slot is created between two sails to pull the boat into the wind. On a run, the sail, or sails, are set more or less perpendicular to the wind.

When the wind is somewhat behind us, I set the boat up with the big genoa poled out to port and the trysail set to port on the boom, somewhat perpendicular to the wind. Having accomplished that, I experiment with the new sail set and Windy's (angle of the wind) set. I put the wind on the beam so that an aerodynamic slot forms between the genoa and the trysail, while the trysail is somewhat perpendicular to act as a running sail. The result is an easy ride with speeds in the six plus knot range, with some seven plus knot surges with the help of a positive current. We hold this speed for over twenty-four hours and think we might be able to go all the way to Trinidad with this sail set.

Great sailing, great fun!

Mon, we're on the Trinidad Express!

Day #43, Wednesday, March 2, 2005
Noon Position: 4 deg. 12 min N, 44 deg. 22 min W
1,100 nautical miles to Trinidad
Noon-to-Noon Run: 150 nautical miles

Jim flaking the mainsail to secure for night.

Good days can follow one another. We have another fantastic one hundred fifty nautical-mile run in beautiful weather.

Day #44, Thursday, March 3, 2005
Noon Position: 4 deg. 58 min N, 46 deg. 13 min W
981 nautical miles to Trinidad
Noon-to-Noon Run: 121 nautical miles

At the midnight watch change, I spot a brightly lit oil platform on the horizon ahead. We discuss how well-lit and big they are. Bill retires, but as we approach, I notice the oil platform is moving.

I call, "Captain on Deck."

We watch as the ship (a fishing vessel?) runs down our starboard side, turns, and takes up station on our starboard aft quarter. He then charges, at high speed, directly towards us. We start the diesel and motor sail away as quickly as possible. The ship slows and finally falls astern.

Bill has never seen such behavior. He speculates that they must have thought we were going to poach their fishing territory. Later during the watch, when I spot another fishing vessel, I keep a greater distance.

The weather clears about noon, and Bill decides it is time to replace the tired, patched 170% genoa with a newer 150% genoa. In addition to the failing fabric patch he had installed earlier, several seams have ripped stitching, allowing light to filter through the sail in unsightly streaks. Ultraviolet light has damaged the fabric so much that the old and new stitching is letting go in long lines along the sail seams. The sail is in danger of ripping right across a panel.

The percentages in the names of the sails are in relation to the space between the mast and headstay, hence a 150% genoa is 1.5 times the size of the mast/headstay triangle.

Bill and I spend two hours on deck in the hot equatorial sun furling the torn 170% genoa and stowing both poles. We redeploy the sail to flop about as we unload it from the roller furling rig onto the deck and tie it temporarily to the lifeline. We load the 150% genoa on the roller furler, furl the sail, reset a pole, and then deploy the new sail.

We pick a time for the sail change when the wind and seas are at a minimum (that's why we picked such a hot time to change the genoa); however, the deck pitches and bucks like normal. Both of us are careful to make sure we are clipped to a hard point and we make our movements slowly and deliberately.

We rest all afternoon to recoup after our roasting on deck.

James E. Keen

 Day #45, Friday, March 4, 2005
Noon Position: 5 deg. 53 min N, 47 deg. 45 min W
875 nautical miles to Trinidad
Noon-to-Noon Run: 106 nautical miles

❧ ❧ ❧

Bill's Email Dispatch

We are about 250 nautical miles offshore moving across the mouth of the Amazon River. I have heard that silt from the Amazon makes the ocean murky, but so far it is just as clear as ever.

We are caught in a countercurrent eddy. The boat feels like it is sailing well but the GPS speed is down in the 3s. With the wind from almost due north, we are on a close reach, motoring and making about 4.5 knots up the line, but the current slows our speed over ground to about 3 knots. This is not good!

Our weather guy is Herb Hilgenberg, of Southbound II, a ship routing and weather forecasting service located in Burlington, Ontario, Canada. Herb is well known to east coast sailors—a legend with his helpful service. We have not contracted for personalized service. However, Herb checks in with a forecast for Arjumand and Tramontana, two vessels that are near. They confirm his forecast answering that it is hot, humid, and difficult sailing.

❧ ❧ ❧

The winds freshen overnight to a mini-blow. Walking, sleeping, doing anything below is almost impossible. It's like being inside a clothes washer. My bunk is above where the bow slams repeatedly into waves so sleeping is almost impossible.

In spite of the furious motion, I make fish cakes for lunch in an effort to use eggs. We eat on the Veranda while ducking cascades of

212

spray that wash down the gunwale onto the deck where it smashes into the combing and sends water streaming into the cockpit. We're wet, but it's cooler in the cockpit than roasting in the steaming hot cabin.

We consume our last Fernando melon for dinner. It is not very ripe or good.

James E. Keen

Day #46, Saturday, March 5, 2005
Noon Position: 6 deg. 56 min N, 49 deg. 20 min W
763 nautical miles to Trinidad
Noon-to-Noon Run: 112 nautical miles

❦ ❦ ❦

Bill's Email Dispatch

Last night was busy, not just sitting and letting the boat sail herself. The sea was very choppy and once actually tossed Jim out of his bunk. It was total overcast with showers and wind of 20 knots. The boat is bouncing and spray is flying. The knot meter is broken so I do not know how fast we were going, but it felt we were going faster than the GPS speed of 3.5 knots. The boat's true heading was 330°, but the course made good was 300° so there must have been a current swirl.

Previously, we have sailed around the world either on a port tack or running before the wind. On Advent II, nothing works on a starboard tack. The sink near the bow overflows, the settee/dinette seat is on the high side so you fall out of it, and the galley stove is on the low side so you fall into it. When sitting at the chart table, I fall into the companionway area instead of being able to lean against the cabinetry. And, worst of all, instead of being pushed into his bunk, Jim is tossed out of it.

But, today things are nearly perfect. The sun is shining for a change, and we are making 5.5 knots on a good course. The sea has calmed, and all is well. That's like the sea!

❦ ❦ ❦

The Trinidad Express returns and we have one of our better sailing days. The humidity drops and life is better.

214

There are no signs of civilization except for the sounds of the SSB radio. The nights are absolutely black. A puny third quarter moon rises, but is lost among the thick clouds that block all starlight. Black night sailing is scary but beautiful. Facing a four-hour watch alone on a black night is still daunting.

But, Mon, we are on the Trinidad Express!

James E. Keen

Day #47, Sunday, March 6, 2005
Noon Position: 8 deg. 8 min N, 51 deg. 2 min W
641 nautical miles to Trinidad
Noon-to-Noon Run: 122 nautical miles

✦ ✦ ✦

<u>*Bill's Email Dispatch*</u>

Clear sunny sky, light wind, sailing about 4 knots. The computer charts, Herb, and the people we talk to on the radio, all say that there is a strong positive current out here, but we haven't found it.

✦ ✦ ✦

We have smooth sailing in the morning but start the engine at 1530 hours. It is a very calm day with diminishing wind. We're about one hundred eighty nautical miles offshore and find counter current eddies in reverse of the big offshore current (similar to the counter currents of the Gulf Stream that are often encountered while sailing off the U.S. east coast).

Bill is listening to Herb give custom weather/current predictions to other boats. Herb uses satellite weather prediction charts to craft specific forecasts under contract. We don't have a custom forecast, but Bill's listening to forecasts for nearby boats to interpolate our weather.

Trinidad Express

Day #48, Monday, March 7, 2005
Noon Position: 8 deg. 45 min N, 52 deg. 47 min W
547 nautical miles to Trinidad
Noon-to-Noon Run: 94 nautical miles

✄   ✄   ✄

Bill's Email Dispatch

We have sailed out of one weather system into another. For weeks we have had clouds with frequent showers. Now the sky is clear, the horizon is Carolina Blue, and overhead is Duke Blue. Last night the sky was full of stars. All my life I have been vaguely aware of the North Star, and known that it is hard to see. For some reason, here it is obvious—follow the Big Dipper pointers and there it is, 8° above the horizon. And the Southern Cross is at home opposite the Big Dipper, high in the southern sky.

We are sailing at a very smooth 5.5 knots. This will put us into Trinidad on Saturday if conditions hold, but it is irrational to think that we will sail at 5.5 knots for the next 5 days.

✄   ✄   ✄

Day #49, Tuesday, March 8, 2005
Noon Position: 9 deg. 20 min N, 55 deg. 7 min W
404 nautical miles to Trinidad
Noon-to-Noon Run: 143 nautical miles

❧ ❧ ❧

<u>Bill's Email Dispatch</u>

I have just realized that this journey is rapidly coming to an end. If I have anything profound to say I had better get it out. I'll put them in categories of Things, People, and Places.

THINGS:

- *Of course, the big thing is the boat, Advent II. I have nothing but good to say about her. She sails well, is comfortable, dry, easy to control, predictable, and very strong. That is the big picture. Now for some parts:*
- *Windpilot steering wind vane (Windy): Excellent*
- *Simrad electric autopilot: Surprisingly good. We only use it when motoring so it did not have to deal with the constantly changing forces of sailing. At times, like motoring out False Bay in South Africa, it had to work hard dealing with the wind and waves. It always did the job well. We have had problems with the belt alignment. The plastic brackets seem to bend with age and use, resulting in bad alignment. Three times this misalignment caused the belt retainer and belt to come off, and we went around in circles.*
- *Vetus 62 horsepower diesel engine (Leo): I do not know why Vetus does not market their engines in the U.S. This is a good engine. It starts quickly and runs well whether it is under heavy load, as for the Panama Canal transit, or at low RPMs for six days nonstop. We ran it 1,400 hours total. Fuel consumption was 0.4 gallons per hour at slow cruise of about 4 knots. The fuel system for this engine is self-purging. Just*

218

crank the starter and it expels air from the system. A great feature. Another great feature is the built-in oil removal pump. To change oil, just stick the little hose in an empty oil container, and pump out the old oil. I do not dump waste oil at sea. I carry it around for thousands of miles until we find a proper dump site. Buying oil filters has been a problem.

- *Fuel: We never had any fuel problems. There is a vacuum gauge on the fuel line that monitors the condition of the filter. I changed the fuel filter only one time. We carried three plastic fuel jerry jugs on the rail, filled. These did add to the fuel on board, however, the real reason for them was to transport fuel from ashore. Fuel docks are few and far between. When refueling time came, we would empty the jugs into the ship's tank. Almost always there would be black slime in the bottoms of the jugs. We took care to seal the jugs to prevent water entry, and always covered them from the sun and direct spray, and even used biocide some of the time. The worst of it was in fuel we bought in Morehead City, North Carolina. Does that mean that fuel in the U.S. is contaminated? No. I think that most of the problems blamed on contaminated foreign fuel really originate onboard. I think we grow our own fuel problems. One of the many good features of Advent II is that the keel is the fuel tank. It always stays the temperature of the surrounding water, which is more stable than the air temperature. I think this reduces the moisture that enters, and eliminates water-related fuel problems. There is a spin-on Racor fuel filter that is a mess to change. I guess if I did it more than once every two years, I would figure out how to do it and not make a mess.*
- *Transmission: Hurth. No problems, I like it. The good thing is that I let the propeller spin. There is no need for a shaft brake or folding prop. Drag is very low. I do wish I could use that spinning shaft to generate electricity.*
- *Solar panels: Siemens (Shell Energy) four each, 55 watts each. I am very happy with them. The stated ampere capacity is 3.15,*

and on a sunny day, that much is produced. They are mounted above the bimini. The location is good. They generate enough electricity for almost all our needs. I never expected to use the computer so much, and I never thought a laptop computer used so much electricity. The computer really digs deep into the energy budget. With minimal computer use, the solar panels keep the batteries charged. If the computer is used a lot for composing, email, weatherfax, grib files, electronic plotting, route planning, etc., we run about 20 amp hours a day negative. About every four days we have to run the engine to recharge the batteries. The daily electricity consumption is about 70 amp hours. Cloudy days will require more frequent use of the engine. We have never been short of energy at anchor. I think the alternator is about 100 amps. At 1,200 rpm engine speed and the batteries down 100 amp hours, the charge rate is 50 amps, and it declines as the batteries charge. Running the engine two or three hours every few days is a terrible way to charge batteries. I would love to have a shaft generator. The voltage regulator is not the highly hyped three stage but is an ordinary two stage. It was recommended by Hamilton Ferris, where I bought the alternator and regulator. The batteries charge at whatever the alternator will put out up to 14.3 volts and then the regulator limits the charge to what the batteries will accept at 14.3 volts, which is about 4 amps. I have four batteries, bought at H&H Golf Carts in Chocowinity. When I motor for days on end, I continually put 1 amp of electricity into each battery (at 14.3 volts). It doesn't hurt the lead acid batteries, and I see no need for an expensive, complicated three stage regulator.

- A Prowatt 1000 inverter provides 120-volt AC for computers, charging flashlight batteries, VHF, hair clippers, video camera, etc. The primary reason for it was to drive the angle grinder for steel and paint repair. The largest current draw is a small shop vacuum, which is really nice to have. We burned *up several smaller inverters before we started using the larger one.*

- *In hot areas, cabin fans are great. We have several cheap auto fans which work well, although they interfere with email transmission. One or more of these fans is running almost all the time. We also have one expensive Caframo marine fan. It is two speed, uses less electricity, is quieter, and does not mess up radio use.*
- *There is a 3 burner Force 10 galley stove, which is a joy. The little spark thing stopped working so now we light it with a propane grill lighter.*
- *I still like the composting head (Virginia).*
- *The radio (SSB) is an ICOM M710, with an SCS PCT-IIe pactor TNC for email. Good equipment.*
- *We have a 110-pound Bruce anchor with 400 feet of 5/16 HT chain. The Bruce will not cut through grass, and it scoops up cobbles instead of digging through, but no anchor is perfect. I am happy with the ground tackle.*
- *The genoa is the sail workhorse. When running downwind it is paired with the drifter, both on poles. The other workhorse is the main trysail. We almost never use the big mainsail. The staysail was used only infrequently, probably because it is inconvenient.*
- *The folding dinghy continues to do everything asked of it. It has room, and capacity for people, provisions, fuel and water jerry jugs, and the occasional fisherman who needs a lift out to his boat. It rows easily and will plane one person with a four horsepower motor. It is almost indestructible.*
- *The Johnson outboard motor has surprising power and has run well. The plastic cowl and steering handle feel flimsy, but it has held together. It starts easily and reliably.*

THINGS *that have given up:*

- *The combination depth sounder/knot meter. First the sounder, then the knot meter. I hate combination instruments.*
- *An ICOM HT VHF.*
- *The GPS. We now use a backup handheld unit. It is inconvenient because it is made for land/highway use, not boat use.*
- *An electric autopilot.*
- *Several computers (old used IBM laptops).*
- *Wind speed indicator.*
- *Computer keyboard.*
- *Two steering cables broke. They were original, and I think they broke because the cable size was too large for the pulleys.*
- *I don't know if I wrote about the Profurl bearings going bad. We got to Simon's Town, Normandie left; I started checking on things and discovered that the Profurl would not turn. The bearings had gone bad. Replacements were available from Profurl and were impressively easy to replace.*

PEOPLE:

I read someone's account. They were writing about all the exotic places they had been, and all the experiences. Then they said that the most wonderful thing about cruising is the community of yachties. And they went on to discuss how wonderful yachties are . . .

However:

I think of a yachtie as someone who is traveling around on a boat— Normandie and I are yachties. Yachties may travel just little distances or very long distances, may stay somewhere for a year or so, but they move around. Those wonderful yachties are just another us.

This adventure is drawing to a close. In a few months, we will have resumed normal lives. A part of me does not want to stop. We've done this, and we have gotten good at it. Our identity has changed from our previous occupation to yachtie. We can go anywhere. "Hey Normandie, let's go to the Mediterranean for a few months. . ." We have the knowledge, the experience, and the boat to do it. We can go anywhere.

Where do we want to go? We want to go and see the native people that are important to us—not just other yachties.

I want to go back to see Dash, Normandie's fishing buddy in Tobago. He could not understand us not coming back. "We are friends. You must come back and see Dash."

I want to go find Bud on Gonzo who befriended us in Margarita.

I want to go back to the oyster and pearl people and take them some sugar, dried milk, and lip balm.

I want to go back to see Moses, the world's only windsurfing Kuna Indian. We told him we would come back. We didn't.

I want to go back to see the young man who lived with his family far down a dirt road in Panama. He invited us into his home and gave us fruit juice. We also told him we would be back. We didn't go back.

I want to see Sandy and the cats, the retired veterinarian on Little Bit. I want to see Owen and Betty on Hiatus.

I want to go back to Colon and see Father Panton, the rector at the Anglican Church. In the short time there we became friends. He is black, about ten years younger than I. He was an exchange student at Broughton High School in Raleigh, North Carolina. That is where I went to school. Had he been my age, in the days of segregation, he could not have gone to Broughton. Now we are friends. Things are better now.

I want to go back to Galapagos and see Rufus.

I want to go back to Australia. Jan and Dave befriended us, and in the process let us know a little piece of Australia. And Greg and Robyn, more church friends, who also lived on the hook and who looked after my transportation needs.

And after a few years, I want to go back and see Louie, the friend in Simon's Town who so passionately believes that South Africa can be a moral leader in the world.

PLACES:

It comes as a shock to self-centered Americans; there is a world out there! I have always thought of my little blue U.S. passport as granting me some sort of special consideration. Nope! If anyone has special consideration, it is Commonwealth citizens, not U.S. citizens. Even if U.S. policies are largely disapproved of by the rest of the world, they do genuinely like Americans.

However, some, notably the French, didn't like Americans but did like us. Most of the people we met had either been to the U.S. or someone close to them had. By way of the news, television, and personal experience, the general knowledge of the U.S. is quite high and quite accurate. I always found it somewhat flattering for someone who hardly spoke English to identify me as being from the South. They discerned different U.S. accents.

Generally, the U.S. is the force to be reckoned with. Others may love or hate it, but the U.S. had to be considered. However, China is now becoming a party that has to be considered. China is taking manufacturing jobs from all countries, not just the U.S. And China is now investing in other countries, so I guess the big takeover has started. This influence is being felt mostly in the Asian subcontinent, but also the Pacific, east Africa, and to some extent Australia.

Something has happened on the world stage that I was only vaguely aware of. I did know that there is something called the European Union. I did know that there was a lot of talk about a common currency. But, thought I, France will never give up their franc. Germany will never give up the mark or Italy their lire. Well, they have. We were in

Polynesia on EU Election Day. Many places were closed. What is so important about EU elections? What do people have to vote for? They were voting on their representatives to the EU. It is a law making body. It has authority to make binding law on the not-so-sovereign states. That boggles my mind.

The EU has the authority to make labor laws for all the members. And what's more, the people we talked to are very enthusiastic about the EU. Boats are flying EU ensigns. What you see is the old national flag, but in the upper left corner, similar to the U.S. flag, is a blue field with a circle of stars. That blue with the circle of stars is the EU flag.

U.S. citizens are required to have a visa before entering French Polynesia. The visa was easily obtained at the French Embassy in Panama City. We made three visits to the French Embassy. Flying proudly over the French Embassy is not the Blue, White and Red French tricolor, but the new French/European Union flag. The combined European Union has a larger economy than the U.S.

Around the world, there is a coming together of countries with similar interests. The Caribbean Community, The Pacific Nations, Southeast Asia, and South Africa, the unquestioned leader of sub-Sahara Africa. Kenya, Tanzania, and Uganda have just joined in an economic zone. I heard last week that several South American countries are coming together. And then there are powerhouses like Brazil and India that are just beginning to emerge. I do not know what all this means except that there is a world out there that is changing. No longer is the U.S. here, Europe there, and Japan over there. The U.S. is one of many. And I heard on BBC that China just bought the laptop division from IBM.

We were in Panama, clustered with a group of yachties as usual. The talk of the group was that some of them were going down the coast of South America, then up a river to a village where the people still live traditionally and really do welcome visiting yachts. We couldn't go because we were heading somewhere else. All across the Pacific we constantly had to skip places because we were going somewhere else.

In Tahiti, we made the big decision and had a big realization. We had to decide whether to keep going west (sail for America), or to take our time and see more of the Pacific (New Zealand and Australia). The big decision was to sail west. We have been to many strange and beautiful places and have met wonderful people. Sailing west would limit the places and people we would encounter. We started talking about the places we would have to come back to next time. Then we had a big realization: you can't visit them all. We could spend a lifetime and there would still be more places to see and people to meet. But we had seen some.

We knew what it was like to sail into a new harbor, just like the sailors of old, the same harbors. And people still come out to greet you just as they did then. And they want to know you, they welcome you, and they do not want you to go, just as in times past. We could not see them all, but we had seen some.

And that made it okay to gather our memories and go home.

All of the people I want to go back to see are local people, local boat lovers, or boat people. These are not yachties. Yes, I would love to meet up with yachtie friends again, but when you say goodbye to a yachtie you both know that the friendship you have is good, it may be renewed someday, and that there will be others. A yachtie is just another you, going somewhere else. Some yachties stay close to the group, make passages part of a group, and go to the anchorages with others of the group. I think these are the people who think that the best thing about cruising is the community of yachties. I disagree. I think it is the other people out there you get to know, and love.

🌀　🌀　🌀

The great wind continues today with the Advent II Reach and Run sail plan producing speeds at times in excess of seven knots. It's a beautiful, cloudless, eighty-eight-degree day with low humidity.

Bill thinks we may have a chance of arriving late on Friday; otherwise, we'll have to spend the night offshore for a Saturday arrival. Galleon's Passage, between Trinidad and Tobago, and Dragon's Mouth (the entrance to The Gulf of Paria) near Chaguaramas harbor are studded with peril. The Dragon Mouth passage is very narrow and we need good daylight to attempt entering the harbor.

James E. Keen

Day #50, Wednesday, March 9, 2005
Noon Position: 10 deg. 16 min N, 57 deg. 19 min W
264 nautical miles to Trinidad
Noon-to-Noon Run: 140 nautical miles

🌀 🌀 🌀

Bill's Email Dispatch

Our wonderful wind and current have gone and we are motoring. Other than that, everything is wonderful; beautiful sun, calm seas, and two more days to Trinidad.

🌀 🌀 🌀

After a night of good sailing and tangling with four fishing boats, the wind dies completely and a negative current eddy won't let the boat go much above five knots under power and sail. We're under a running sail plan now, wing-n-wing with the genoa and mainsail. It's going to be downhill and downwind all the way to Trinidad.

Bill's making bread again today, but the yeast he's using is at least a year out of date and we have not heeded the "refrigerate after opening" requirement. Last Monday's bread rose about half what it should. Oh well!

Do you realize what good asparagus we have in the U.S.? Even the canned stuff is good. I made a one-pot meal yesterday and opened a can of asparagus from South Africa. The green sticks were about half an inch in diameter, pasty-white in color, and absolutely tasteless. I need U.S. asparagus.

* * * * * *

I've had a stuffy nose all my life, but out here at sea, my sinusitis has completely disappeared—until today.

228

Did I get a virus from email?

Ha, ha! That's the kind of joke you can expect after weeks of confinement on a thirty-six foot sailboat!

Trinidad, oh Trinidad!

Bill wants ice cream. I want a shower—a real, everlasting, hot shower!

James E. Keen

Day #51, Thursday, March 10, 2005
Noon Position: 10 deg. 56 min N, 59 deg. 22 min W
142 nautical miles to Trinidad
Noon-to-Noon Run: 122 nautical miles

We need to check in on Friday as the weekend brings overtime charges from the customs officials. We're charging ahead as fast as possible as Bill wants his ice cream bad!

After lunch yesterday, I cleaned the pressure cooker pot and put in dried black-eyed peas, green peas, and water. I brought it up to pressure and left it overnight. Today, I opened the pot, added meat and reheated it for a normal one-pot meal.

When I served it, Bill asked, "Where's the rice?"

I had made a one-pot meal without rice! Despite Bill's comments, it was good. We both had second servings and there were no leftovers.

The sloppy weather continues, so does the drone of the diesel. The whole boat vibrates with noise, but we are closing on Trinidad, Mon!

230

Day #52, Friday, March 11, 2005
Noon Position: 10 deg. 49 min N, 61 deg. 27 min W
15 nautical miles to Trinidad
Noon-to-Noon Run: 129 nautical miles

❧   ❧   ❧

Bill's Email Dispatch

Anchor down, Chaguaramas, Trinidad at1500 hours.

❧   ❧   ❧

When I arrive for the midnight watch, ships' lights are everywhere. The Captain keeps the helm. As I watch, he identifies and avoids four or five ships converging on the northeast corner of Trinidad. The glow of an oil production platform with three visible drilling towers is from a tremendous natural gas flare; it literally brightens the sky for hundreds of square miles. It will take until the end of my watch at 0400 hours to pass this huge wasteful monument to the energy economy of Trinidad. Why can't they use all that natural gas instead of just burning it off?

At the 0400 hours watch change, Galera Point on the northeast corner of Trinidad comes into view. From that point, it takes most of the daylight hours to negotiate the forty-two miles of the Caribbean Ocean pass between Trinidad and Tobago and into the Bocas del Dragon (Dragon's Mouth), a narrow pass that leads to the Gulf of Paria.

We spend the day sailing west, two or three miles off the Trinidad coast. It is a rough coastline with cliffs rising from the beach to a high mountainous ridgeline on the horizon.

We sail past several groups of fisherman; two in a boat, trolling for fish, while a larger boat stands by to transport the big catch. These eighteen-foot boats have raised elongated bows, a classic signature of Trinidad boats. Most are painted with custom bright colorful patterns but are always painted turquoise inside.

231

Dragon's Mouth is roughly two hundred feet wide, squeezed between almost vertical cliffs. It's as if the mountain had been cleaved with a large axe, leaving a slice that the ocean rushes through. Large scars of exposed rock mark where landslides have cleared trees from the steep slopes. At one point, a small island has been created by the rushing current. It has raw earthen sides with trees still growing on the top awaiting the erosion that will cause them to plunge into the maelstrom. Cliffs become more vertical and the current increases as the passage width shrinks. Then the passage opens, to reveal a mini-bay on the starboard where sailboats are moored. We can see the end of the cut where the Gulf of Paria begins. The slope becomes gentler and houses cluster near the shoreline.

We turn to port along the mountainous mainland shoreline. Suddenly, we are in traffic; a six-pack dive boat, a large aluminum cruising sloop, and a runabout. The channel takes us between the mountainous mainland and mountainous islands. Houses cling to both shorelines with others scattered on green hillsides.

In the waterway ahead, there is a shipyard to port where a large dry docked oil drilling rig towers over the yard. Large shipyard buildings crowd around the dry dock and we can hear the din of heavy machinery.

Masts of moored sailboats seem to block our path in the distance with a large ship docked behind the sailboats. In the distance are low mountains and steep mountain islands are nearer on the starboard. Wide passages between the islands lead to the open gulf. You can almost see the mountainous Venezuelan coast as it hides in the clouds on the horizon a scant six miles away. Venezuela's famous Orinoco River and delta is to the southwest.

We have arrived at Chaguaramas Harbor, Trinidad, eight full days ahead of our original ETA of March 19. We have tickets for an airline flight home on March 17, giving us six lay days to enjoy the island. Bill can finally relax from his fear of standing up Grayson at the altar.

You might say that our Trinidad Express has arrived!

Chapter 7

Trinidad: Energy Powerhouse,

Voodoo Society

Trinidad is the larger of two islands that make the island nation of Trinidad and Tobago. It is the southernmost of the Caribbean islands and lies just seven miles off the coast of Venezuela. In 1498, Christopher Columbus renamed the island La Isla de la Trinidad (The Island of the Trinity).

The island has an area of 1,864 square miles and is the fifth largest island in the West Indies. Looking like a squared backward C, the island has mountains along the northern shoreline, several small mountain ranges, great swamps, and major inland plains on the southern part of the island.

The upper westward-pointing part of the C is the mountainous Chaguaramas Peninsula. The southern westward-pointing part of the C, south of the country's largest city of San Fernando, is sparsely populated. Most people avoid this area as an uninteresting and desolate farming, fishing, and oil production peninsula. Cedros and Icacos are towns in this remote area.

Unstable sands, mud volcanoes, and La Brea Pitch Lake, one of three asphalt lakes in the world, are found here. Sir Walter Raleigh is said to have used tar from the lake to caulk his ships. Tar has been mined there since 1859 with the British Empire using it worldwide for road construction, a practice that continues today. Eagles have been seen cooking their catch on the hot tar lake surface.

The Gulf of Paria separates Trinidad from Venezuela.

* * * * * *

Arawaks and Caribs inhabited the islands in prerecorded history. Trinidad was a Spanish colony but largely inhabited by French colonists. In 1889, the British united Trinidad and Tobago into a single Crown Colony, and it remained so until it gained self-government in 1958. It became a republic in 1976.

Port of Spain, the capital city of Trinidad and Tobago, is located on the Gulf of Paria. Chaguaramas, a peninsula located west of Port of Spain, was leased to the U.S. Navy in 1940 for the construction of a naval base. In early 1956, that base was scaled back, and in the 1960s it was used as a missile tracking station in the BEMEWS (Ballistic Missile Early Warning Tracking System). In 1963, the entire peninsula was returned to the Trinidad and Tobago government. Today, the port is a repair facility for oil and gas platforms and used for shipment of oil field supplies. It also has become a major yachting supply and storage center.

The country has a large industrial and agricultural economy based largely on oil and natural gas. It is a leading exporter of ammonia and liquefied natural gas.

San Fernando and Chaguanas are larger than Port of Spain. However, Port of Spain has an important port for the shipment of container freight, oil, and natural gas.

Our Island Visit

Chaguaramas Bay: Deepwater Chaos

At 1500 hours, Advent II is tied to the customs dock along with other boats waiting for inspection. It will take a while. Maybe we should go to a mooring.

Chaguaramas Harbor, Trinidad. Shipyards on left with anchorage in middle.

We are at the top of sheltered Chaguaramas harbor, a refuge bay that is surrounded by small mountains. Deep water makes the harbor ideal for berthing large oil platform service ships that move about at all hours.

Next to where we are docked is the pyramid shaped building housing the Crews Inn, a complex of shops and restaurants that cater to cruisers. Across a spit of water are repair and storage boatyards for cruising sailors, commercial yards for large ships needing replenishment and repair, and the shipyard.

Nearby is a huge warehouse next to a concrete dock where long lengths of drilling pipe are stacked awaiting loading onto an oil platform supply ship. Other supplies are being hoisted aboard a long low black ship that has rust stains visible along the scarred painted topside. I can see racks of drilling pipe already securely lashed on the deck of the ship.

We move Advent II to the sailboat anchorage area and pick up mooring #17, a short distance abeam of the service vessel.

Building the dinghy is much easier this time, and it's in the water in short order. As Bill pilots Shirley to the customs dock to finalize our entry, I tidy up our filthy boat. She has served us well on our 52-day crossing from South Africa.

* * * * * *

Bill returns after a bit and says, "They need to see you!"

I jump into Shirley and we motor back to the customs dock. I stand in front of an immigration officer who, after a cursory look, dismisses me with a wave. I'm disappointed that I only merit one short, live, visible check. Undaunted, I walk down the dock to explore Crews Inn. Bill stays behind to do the paperwork and move on to customs for more paperwork.

I find a convenience store and lust for beer and Snickers. But, I have no local money and the clerk refuses to take my U.S. dollars. The Trinidad and Tobago currency is the TTD (6 Trinidad and Tobago dollars per U.S. dollar in 2005), although locals use the term TT. Next door is an internet shop where I convince the clerk to trade TTs for dollars. Back at the convenience store, I flaunt my TTs at the boorish clerk.

Bill finds me before I buy the beer and Snickers. We instead buy ice cream cones and lounge about a store that is overstuffed with merchandise crowding the narrow aisles. Later we buy a bag of ice, the first since I've been aboard, and head back to the boat to have iced drinks on the forecastle.

By 1900 hours, we're asleep.

Day #53, Saturday, March 12, 2005
Chaguaramas Bay, Trinidad

At 0600 hours I find Bill sitting on the foredeck in a lawn chair. I join him for coffee and silence as we enjoy the sights and sounds of an awakening commercial and yachting harbor.

Small mountains rise directly from the depths of Chaguaramas Harbor to frame the northern skyline. As a former U.S. Naval Base, the harbor is deep enough that anchoring is not a good idea. Our mooring is attached to a large weight sunk into the harbor bottom, giving good holding, even in adverse conditions. Our own anchor would be insufficient at best with the short slope of the rode in the seventy-five foot deep water.

The commercial shipyard at the west end of the harbor provides round-the-clock work and noise. Crew boats, often one hundred fifty feet in length, come and go at all hours from the oil rig service yard just to our east. In between are yachting facilities that provide full service and yard storage for visiting yachts. Our anchorage is in the middle of the harbor where all the action (and noise) takes place.

Trinidad is located south of the hurricane belt, just sixty miles south of Grenada at the south end of the danger area. Trinidad is considered a safe refuge for the hurricane season. Insurance companies discount their rate when a boat is moved out of the hurricane zone, so cruising boats migrate to Trinidad during the dangerous season. Life is easy and many just get stuck here.

* * * * * *

The task for the day: laundry. I stuff two bulging bunches of smelly clothes into bags and ride Shirley to the Laundromat. Washing clothes occupy my morning, and then, anticipating that long hot shower, I take a cold-water shower instead.

Yes, cold water—the preferred way in Trinidad.

A hot shower leaves you steamy and sticky. In the cold shower method, you get wet, lather up, rinse, lather again, and rinse a final time. It's nice, not sticky, and refreshing. Besides, the water is not really cold as it is stored in big blue above ground tanks where the sun provides some warmth. My endless hot shower, the one that I dreamed about on those long watch hours, becomes a cold shower that really is best in the tropics.

We putter about for the afternoon and have an early evening barbecue pork chop dinner at a waterfront authentic tropical restaurant in the nearby Power Boats complex. The crowd is a lively mix of locals and cruisers.

We head for the boat and the bunk.

Day #54, Sunday, March 13, 2005
Chaguaramas Bay, Trinidad

Port of Spain: Architecture and Drinking Nuts

Bill and I meet again on the foredeck to watch the sun rise. Bill suggests we should go to church in Port of Spain. We need to leave soon.

We catch a Maxi Taxi (5TT, US$0.80) minivan and share the ride with several other passengers. These taxis have no schedule, leave the stop when they are full, and follow a fixed route. Our taxi takes us past old navy buildings that have been transformed into marine service businesses. The steep slope of a mountain is on the left while neatly trimmed lawns decorate the area between shoreline buildings on the right. We pass through the open entrance gates next to the unoccupied former U.S. Naval Base entrance checkpoint where neatly trimmed shrubbery surrounds a big sign announcing the Chaguaramas Marine Center.

Outside the old navy base, the character of buildings changes to a seedier, but colorful, look. Neatly trimmed lawns, so common on the old base, are replaced with stark concrete sidewalks. Colorfully painted concrete block walls provide security for the colorful stucco-on-concrete block houses. Iron gates pierce security walls that provide some noise abatement from the din of traffic.

The road, Western Main Street, follows the shoreline of the bay. I can occasionally see water between patches of mixed commercial and residential buildings. We pass docks and marinas as the road curves south.

After a ten-minute ride, Bill announces we should get off. We step onto the sidewalk near a power station in a blighted area surrounded by walled houses and businesses. Bill immediately realizes we have gotten off the taxi too soon. We start walking toward our destination, about a mile away. I later find this seedy neighborhood is just like many others in Port of Spain.

At this early morning hour, we encounter few residents on the walk to Queen's Park Savannah. Those 260 acres of open parkland are surrounded by large oak trees that line the world's largest traffic roundabout (that's the claim). At 2.2 miles long, the roundabout forms a tree-lined rectangle around the deserted open grass park.

The park has been a sugar cane field and alternately used as a cattle pasture. In recent times, the neighborhood has become more upscale as the home for the Savannah Race Track and several athletic fields. To the north of the park are the Royal Botanic Gardens, The Emperor Valley Zoo, and the President's house.

On the southern side of the savannah is the grandstand, used in the past for viewing horse races. It's now used as a viewing stand for the world famous Carnival parade. The Port of Spain National Academy of the Arts is an architecturally pleasing building, and Memorial Park and the Knowsley Minister of Foreign Affairs building are neighbors.

The western side of the savannah is home to the Magnificent Seven—world class structures that include: Queen's Royal College; Stollmeyer's Castle; homes for the Anglican Bishop, the Roman Catholic Archbishop and the Prime Minister; Whitehall (Prime Minister's office); and Mille Fleurs, a French provincial style estate.

The American Embassy and our church destination are adjacent, about halfway along the western side of the savannah lawn.

* * * * * *

The All Saints Anglican Church is magnificent in a rustic way. Built of plastered rubble stone with Gothic arch windows trimmed in a lighter stone, the corners have flying buttress-like attachments in the lighter stone. A black slate roof has small iron crosses at each gable.

All Saints Anglican Church.

The traditional interior has stone floors and plain wooden pews, an ornate ceiling with open wood trusses, and is illuminated by the huge stained glass windows on the savannah end of the long open sanctuary. Ornate wood carvings decorate areas of the white stucco walls.

The congregation is just as traditional with ladies dressed in fashionable finery and large hats. The men are equally well dressed and greet guests and each other with equal gusto. The priest speaks from his elevated pulpit.

A large crowd attends the preferred 0730 hours service. The middle of the day is just too hot, so the early morning services are popular.

We are recognized as visitors along with about fifteen or twenty others. I take this as a sign of a healthy congregation. There is a very dignified British man, another not so British looking but just as British man, and Bill and me as white face standouts in the black congregation. We are welcomed heartily by the powerful, heavily accented voice of the priest.

The singing is great, the sermon understandable, and the people very welcoming and friendly.

James E. Keen

A drinking nut vendor in front of All Saints Anglican Church.

* * * * * *

In the crowd outside the church after the service, we watch children play on the small lawn next to a narrow street separating the church from the U.S. Embassy. The street has been partially closed where a big concrete barrier prevents vehicles from closely approaching the high steel picket security fence of the embassy. Vehicles picking up or discharging passengers at the side entrance of the church are crowded. Bill said the partial street closing has caused problems for the church, a fact he learned when he and Normandie visited at the start of their circumnavigation.

We cross Maraval Road in front of the church to the savannah where a drinking coconut vendor had set up shop. Coconuts provide a

242

natural cool drink of water that is favored in tropical latitudes. A tall slender bearded man wearing a baseball cap is selling the drinking nuts from the back of his blue pickup truck. An eagle drawing splashes across the hood while coconut tree drawings adorn the truck's doors. A towering steel cage, filling the back of the truck, is crammed with green and yellow coconuts.

As a crowd gathers, the vendor climbs on his wooden platform alongside the truck and reaches into the pile to select a coconut. He uses his machete to lop off its top and offers the bowl-shaped nut, with cool sweet water inside, to customers. We drink and return the nut to the vendor. He slices more to reveal the meaty interior of the coconut with a thin slimy coating to be scraped off and eaten. Trinidadians consider the solid white coconut meat, which is standard in the U.S., overripe and distasteful; however, they love the slimy young interior of the coconut. It takes considerable nerve for me to taste the treat. It is slimy, almost tasteless, and bland!

* * * * * *

We walk towards the business and waterfront section of Port of Spain but find little early Sunday morning activity. Buildings are short, only one or two stories, except for several high-rise hotels in the nearby port area. There is a seedy feeling and many people we encounter want a handout. I don't feel threatened, but am aware of being watched. We come to Western Main Street, the same wide road we were on earlier, as it runs past the entrance to Kings Wharf Dock at the Port of Trinidad. We can see the tops of large commercial ships, but the activity here is of little interest to us.

We hail a taxi to take us to The Falls at Westmall, a real U.S.-style mall. The taxi drops us on the side of the four-lane road outside a construction and security fence surrounding the mall. A narrow opening, obviously not intended as a pedestrian entrance, allows us to squeeze into the parking lot and we cross towards the almost deserted mall building.

Not only is it too early for stores to be open, construction has closed much of the mall. We see some activity at the end of the building. I ask a lady where we can find a Chinese restaurant. She identifies herself as Angela Richards, an American from Florida.

"None of the restaurants in the mall are open," she says.

She introduces her British husband, Ross Richards, and he says he will take us a few miles down the road to the Ruby Tuesday restaurant. He just needs to make sure that his employees know what to do during his absence.

The Richards are twelve year residents of Trinidad. They run a landscaping business that is installing exterior landscaping, an irrigation system, and interior decorative plants for the mall. I watch Angela apply her light meter to a plant as she explains how hard the mall conditions are for living plants. She has applied a little science and a lot of love to make the plants thrive.

* * * * * *

We arrive at Ruby Tuesday where the building has the same upscale look of those back home and inside, you'd think we were back in the U.S. Ross says he will come in and have a quick drink, but that turns into a three-hour lunch of super hamburgers, conversation, and lots to drink. The air conditioning is almost cold but nice. Glimpses of a television mounted over the bar, where a soccer game is in progress, are almost foreign to us.

Ross explains that he appreciates the chance to have an intelligent conversation. He is very interested in American politics, a Clinton fan, and informative of the political and economic travails of Trinidad. He expresses disbelief in our loyalty to President Bush, an attitude we had heard other times along the way. With reluctance, he excuses himself saying he has to get back to work or face Angela's wrath.

After a few more drinks, we call a taxi for the ride back to Chaguaramas where Shirley takes us back to the boat. We putter the afternoon away and are asleep at our usual 2100 hours.

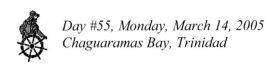

Day #55, Monday, March 14, 2005
Chaguaramas Bay, Trinidad

Monday is a slowdown day as we lounge around the boat until mid-morning. Shirley takes us to the Power Boats boatyard dock where we tie up to do our chores. Bill has to take care of details for the planned haul out, and arrange a much-needed dental appointment.

I lounge about, looking at stored boats. Poking about in a storage yard has always been a favorite pastime where I examine hull shapes, anchoring gear, and other such details. Another cold water shower is delightful, and then I find Hans at the restaurant bar. He and I have several beers and swap stories of our parallel passages from Saint Helena to Fernando, and then Trinidad.

Joy, a singlehanded thrity foot sloop, is easily handled, he says. He sleeps all night with his radar set turned on to detect and warn of approaching ships. He leaves his sails up, unattended, and to the mercy of the wind. He made a short extra stop at Fortaleza, Brazil while we sailed straight to Trinidad, bypassing the Brazilian mainland.

Hans writes for a newspaper and a magazine, telling his readers of his exploits. He has been sailing three and a half years and expects to be out for another two years with a planned trip to the U.S.

Bill finds us and we go to the Roti Shed. The open-air, thatch-roofed shed has bench seating at long common tables for serving the traditional Indian dish that is so prevalent in Trinidad. In the mid-1800s, the British abolished slavery and thousands of Indian citizens were imported to replace slave labor. Today, the Trinidadian society and culture are heavily influenced by the Indian and mixed Indian/black population.

Roti is heavily spiced cubed meat, served with corn and potatoes, and balled-up flat bread that is intended to be used to sop-up the meal.

245

Westerners use a fork and enjoy the bread as a side. Cruisers and workers from the adjacent boatyard vie for available seats for lunch.

Back aboard Advent II, Bill is ready for more adventure.

"Let's go!" he says.

Chacachacare Island: Former Leper Colony

We cast off the mooring buoy and motor sail five miles to the Hansenian Settlement on uninhabited Chacachacare Island. Westernmost of the volcanic Bocas Islands, Chacachacare lies in the *Boca Grande*, the narrow strait between Trinidad and Paria Peninsula of Venezuela. The island was originally named *El Caracol* (the Snail, because of its shape) in 1498 by Christopher Columbus and renamed Chacachacare by Amerindians (American Indians).

U-shaped with a spur, the nine hundred acre national park island is an ancient volcano. One side is blown out, allowing the sea to form a deep-water intrusion. The heavily forested eight hundred sexty five foot mountain almost surrounds the bay and is capped by the 1896 Bocas Lighthouse at La Lve Point. When built, it was the highest above sea level of any other lighthouse in the world. Today the Bocas Lighthouse takes second place to another in Russia. Visitors who climb to the lighthouse can easily see Venezuela.

Since the mid-1800s, a leper colony has existed on the island. Numbering over five hundred patients at a time, victims of the highly contagious Hansen's disease were cared for by Dominican nuns and priests until 1984. New medications eliminated the need for isolation and the island was quickly deserted to become a national park. Trinidadian citizens still avoid the island, fearing the disfiguring infectious disease and ghosts of those who died here.

A plaster-sided leprosarium (hospital) and wood-framed doctor's house sit on the Coco Bay shoreline at the north side of the bay. A multi-story nun's convent and patient's cottages cling to the steep slopes of the south shore on La Chapelle Bay. All the structures have been vandalized and partially reclaimed by nature.

We choose to anchor adjacent to the nun's cottage, some distance from two other yachts intruding on our paradise. Before nightfall, three other boats find their way into the bay, but anchor out of sight to preserve our sense of isolation. We swim in the warm seawater while cleaning algae slime from our boat's hull.

After a fresh water cockpit shower, we ride Shirley to the nearby stone dock where we climb steep steps to encounter a "No Trespassing" sign. After coming this far, we shrug and bypass the sign, continuing to a building prominently outlined on the ridge. Steep concrete steps lead upward through thick brush and knurly trees.

Nun's and Patient's Cottages on Chacachacare Island, Trinidad.

The two-story patient's cottage is perched on the hillside overlooking the bay. Another patient cottages and a nun's residence are farther up the hillside. We go inside where yellow painted rooms, apparently common patient wards with spray painted graffiti on the walls, occupy the first floor. Other rooms are painted pastel blue or green. All the rooms have cathedral style arched top windows with frames that open out to provide free air flow. Several smaller one-patient rooms are on the second floor. A front balcony provides a wonderful view overlooking the rippled blue water of the bay that is framed by the distant tall volcanic ridge.

After picking our way through trash-filled rooms, we go back outside to climb an overgrown, switchback path leading to a carefully tended cemetery. A

Jim surveying well tended cemetery.

rusting wrought iron fence surrounds a dozen rock covered graves. Priests and nuns are remembered on clearly readable headstones with dates ranging from 1870 to 1942. It is a touching scene of lives freely given for the care of others. Someone obviously cares enough to clean these graves to retain their memory among deteriorating abandoned buildings and encroaching scrub forests.

Back aboard our boat, we sit on the foredeck and watch the sky change color. Lengthening shadows darken the mountains as the sun goes down over silent hills filled with the spirits of those who lived and died here.

Bill Doar enjoying the foredeck of Advent II at Chacachacare, Trinidad.

Day #56, Tuesday, March 15, 2005
Chacachacare, Trinidad

☙ ☙ ☙

Bill's Email Dispatch

This is probably my last dispatch. We are safely in Trinidad and Jim and I are flying back to the U.S. on Thursday, March 17. Grayson's wedding is Easter weekend and I will return to Trinidad a week or so after that. I'll paint the bottom of the boat, touch up some rust, and start working my way back to the U.S.

Thank you for joining us on this adventure.

☙ ☙ ☙

We both rise early to sit in silence and enjoy the sunrise.

"When the sun rises over that mountain, it's work time," Bill says in a serious tone.

The sun rises too quickly and a corresponding wind and temperature rise is too much for just sitting on the deck. Using Bill's camera, I take pictures of the scene. We weigh anchor and motor across the windy bay to find sheltered still water for boat chores.

We anchor on the north side in twelve feet of crystal clear water. I climb into Shirley for work on the hull while Bill chooses to swim. We both use Scott Bright pads to clean the hull. Bill cleans the underwater hull while I scrub the topsides along the waterline.

Whenever water splashes on the hull, marine slime grows on the wet area leaving splotchy black slime. It's fairly easy to clean when wet but becomes hard to remove when dry. Since the intent is to haul out Advent II this afternoon, we need to remove as much slime as possible.

250

After a hard hour of hot, slimy work, we take a well-deserved recreational swim by circumnavigating Advent II a few times. A fresh water cockpit shower removes the sea salt and has a cooling effect.

* * * * * *

We motor back to Chaguaramas and pick up our old #17 mooring. Shirley takes us over to Coral Cove where a stop at the Roti shed is first on the list of chores. We eat with Han's Danish friends as he is off doing chores. Bill finalizes haul out arrangements and we go back to the boat at anchorage. Later, we are to move the boat to a Coral Cove slip.

Advent II on Travel Lift before blocking for well deserved rest.

In mid-afternoon, we dock in the Coral Cove travel lift slip and fill the afternoon with preparations for haul out. Following the yard manager's instructions, Bill climbs the mast to remove the twin SSB antennas, effectively cutting our voice and email link with the world. We're ready for our last full day in Trinidad.

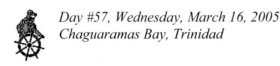

Homeward Bound: Ending the Adventure

This morning, with Bill off to see the dentist, I pack my gear while waiting for the haul out crew. The travel lift arrives, and I watch as Advent II is hoisted and moved ashore to a gravel pad among rows of lonely boats. The process is familiar and straightforward. Advent II is safely blocked by early afternoon. Bill returns and inspects the boat.

Deck equipment is removed and stowed below. Food is checked to avoid spoilage during Bill's planned absence. We'll go to the airport early tomorrow for the flight home. My blue-water adventure has ended.

On our final evening, with preparations complete, Bill and I lounge about the motionless boat. We talk about changes; about how the circumnavigation has changed Bill's and Normandie's lives and what the future will bring. Bill will find another long-term construction project. Normandie is already settled into school and her nursing job. A professional medical career as a Nurse Anesthesiologist is her future.

We speak of my growth as a sailor, about my shrinking waistline and new toughness brought through the constant boat motion. My plans include a circumnavigation of the eastern U.S. by boat—a trip known as America's Great Loop. We talk about how I will resume a normal life with a wife that has allowed me to expand my horizons and to fulfill my dreams of an ocean crossing. We talk about Bill's huge collection of email dispatches and my computer journal. I wonder what we will do with them.

At 2100 hours, just like normal, Bill heads for the bunk.

I sit at the computer and review the file of Bill's dispatches that I intend to use for this book. At the end of the CD listing, I find that Bill has included a quote he collected along the way. I think it's appropriate that he admonishes you (and me) to get off the couch and seek adventure.

Life is like ice.

It goes away whether you use it or not.

James E. Keen

Epilogue

Our flight to Houston, Texas is smooth as is the connecting flight to Raleigh, North Carolina. Jackie and Normandie greet us with smiles. Jackie comments on how much slimmer and tan I look.

What she says has a bit of truth in it. When I flew to South Africa, I had white longish hair and weighed a hefty three hundred pounds. My hair is now a quarter inch buzz cut, still white but on a brightly tanned head. I weigh two hundred fifty pounds, a fifty pound weight loss.

My weight loss secret: a rather restricted diet combined with the constant flexing of muscles while holding onto a wildly shaking boat.

Bill looks normal, tall and slender. He doesn't appear to have changed a bit since I first met him at the Cape Town airport.

We collect our luggage and Normandie retrieves the car for the three-hour ride to our homes. The girls sit in the front and talk and giggle like teenagers.

Bill and I sit in the rear and snore.

* * * * * *

Bill completed his duty at Grayson's wedding by giving away the bride. After visiting with family, he returned to Trinidad. Minor repairs, including bottom paint, made Advent II ready for another ocean voyage.

An island hopping, day sailing adventure led Bill singlehanded through the Caribbean on his boat. After a few months, he arrived home at Chocowinity Bay in North Carolina. He returned to work, signing up for a long-term project in Nigeria, on the west coast of Africa. His new construction project is a huge natural gas gasification plant.

I returned home to Chocowinity for a short reunion with Jackie. She allowed me to start working on a new project of sailing my 32-foot sailing sloop, Irish Mist, on an extended voyage.

On May 7, 2005, I sailed from the Cypress Landing Yacht Club docks near home on a 6,300 mile, 13-month, singlehanded circumnavigation of the eastern United States. This trip is often called America's Great Loop.

Both Advent II and Irish Mist linger on the hard at a local storage yard awaiting new adventure. The two Captains, engaged in daily life, are ready for new adventure!

2016 Update

With my lovely wife Jackie's blessing, I completed the America's Great Loop singlehanded circumnavigation of the U.S. in 13 months. It was a glorious time of sailing with local friends who visited for a short week aboard. Sharing sights with other loopers (as sailors on the loop are called) was a wonderful time.

Visiting America's east coast rivers, spending a substantial time in Canada, following the Mississippi and Ohio rivers and the Tennessee-Tombigbee Canal to the Gulf coast, sailing around the Florida armpit to Key West, to Mexico, and back up the eastern Intracoastal Waterway to home was an adventure of my life that I share in my ebook, *Log of Irish Mist: Cruising America's Great Loop.*

My thirty-two foot sailboat, Irish Mist lingered largely unattended in her slip until I had her hauled to a shipyard where she sat without attention. Finally, after several years of neglect, I sold her to a sailor who is giving her a complete refit.

My sailing life is finished as I volunteer in a local writers group and write about topics generally other than sailing. Personal weight has again become a problem in my sedentary life—up now to 280 pounds. I still wear buzz cut white hair on my balding head along with a white beard that makes me look like Santa Clause.

* * * * * *

Bill finished his tour of duty in Nigeria and then another in Houston before he retired.

After joining Normandie at her new Wilmington, N.C. location and visits with family, he sailed Advent II singlehanded on several trips to southern islands. He recently sailed doublehanded across the Northern Atlantic to circle back to the southern islands in a circumnavigation of the Atlantic Ocean.

I regularly see Advent II at anchor in the Washington, NC harbor waiting for the next adventure.

James E. Keen

Glossary

150% Genoa: A genoa jib sail with a size this is 150% of the triangle between the mast and the forestay.

170% Genoa: A genoa jib sail with a size that is 170% of the triangle between the mast and the forestay.

Abeam: A relative bearing at right angles to the centerline of the ship's keel.

Aft: Toward the stern of the boat.

Amidships: Along the center of the boat.

Astern: Towards the stern (rear) of the boat.

Backstay: A steel cable from the rear of the boat to the masthead, used to support the mast.

Baggywrinkle: A soft covering for lines to reduce sail chafe.

Beam: The width of the vessel at its widest point.

Beating: Sailing as close as possible towards the wind, sometimes in a zig-zag course, to gain upwind direction.

Before the mast: Literally, the area of a ship before the foremast (the forecastle). Most often used to describe men whose living quarters are located here, officers being quartered in the stern-most areas of the ship (near the quarterdeck). Officer-trainees lived between the two ends of the ship and become known as "midshipmen". Crew members who started out as seamen then became midshipmen, and later, officers were said to have gone from "one end of the ship to the other."

Belay: 1. To make fast a line around a fitting, usually a cleat or belaying pin; 2. To secure a climbing person in a similar manner; 3. An order to halt a current activity or countermand an order prior to execution.

Berth: 1. A bed or sleeping accommodation on a boat or ship. 2. A location in a port or harbor used specifically for mooring vessels while not at sea. 3. The safety margin of distance to be kept by a vessel from another vessel or from an obstruction, hence the phrase, "to give a wide berth."

Bilge: The compartment at the bottom of the hull of a ship or boat where water collects and must be pumped out of the vessel.

Binnacle: The stand on which the ship's compass is mounted.

Bitter end: The last part or loose end of a rope or cable.

Block: A pulley or set of pulleys.

Boat: Generally a small marine vessel compared to a ship, a large vessel that carries small boats.

Boatswain Store: A naval supplies store.

Boom: A spar that is attached to the mast and foot of a fore and aft sail.

Bow: The front of the ship.

Bowsprit: A spar projecting from the bow of the boat used for securing anchoring gear. A bowsprit sometimes anchors the bow forestay.

Bridge deck: An upper deck where a ship is steered and the Captain stands; on small yachts, the bridge deck protects the cabin access way.

Brightwork: Exposed varnished wood or polished metal on a boat.

Broach: When a sailing vessel loses control of its motion and is forced into a sudden sharp turn, often heeling heavily and in smaller vessels sometimes leading to a capsize.

Bulkhead: An upright wall within the hull of a ship.

Bulwark: The extension of the ship's side above the level of the weather deck.

Burgee: A small flag, typically triangular, flown from the masthead of a yacht to indicate yacht-club membership.

Cabin: An enclosed room on a deck within a ship or boat.

Capsize: When a ship or boat lists too far and rolls over, exposing the keel.

Catspaws: Light and variable winds on calm waters producing scattered areas of small waves.

Chafing: Wear on line or sail caused by constant rubbing against another surface.

Chine: 1. an angle in the hull. 2. a line formed where the sides of a boat meet the bottom. Soft chine is when the two sides join at a shallow angle, and hard chine is when they join at a steep angle.

Cleat: A stationary device used to secure a rope aboard a vessel.

Clew: The outside corner of a sail.

Close-hauled: A vessel *beating* as close to the wind direction as possible.

Coachroof: The portion of the deck raised to give increased headroom in the cabin.

Coaming: The raised edge of a hatch, cockpit or skylight to help keep out water.

Cockpit: The area towards the stern of a small decked vessel that houses the rudder controls.

Companionway: A raised hatchway in the deck, with a ladder leading below to the main cabin.

Compass: Navigational instrument showing the direction of the vessel in relation to the Earth's geographic or magnetic poles.

Cubby: A small sheltered place on a sailboat.

Dinghy: A type of small boat, often carried or towed for use as a ship's boat by a larger vessel.

Dodger: A lightweight or stout cockpit protection from sea spray or rain.

Doldrums: The equatorial trough with light and variable winds.

Drifter: A very large lightweight sail flown like a jib and used in light wind.

Fiddle: A steel wire bracket used to hold pots securely on the galley stove.

First Mate: The Second in command of a ship.

Flogging: The uncontrolled flapping of sails without being filled with wind.

Following Sea: A wave going in the same direction as a ship.

Forecastle: A partial deck, or foredeck at the head of the vessel, forward of the mast; traditionally the sailors' living quarters. Pronounced fooksel.

Forestays: Long lines or cables, reaching from the bow of the vessel to the mast heads, used to support the mast.

Furl: To roll or gather a sail against its mast or spar.

Galley: The kitchen area of a boat.

Genoa or genny: A large *jib sail*, strongly overlapping the mainmast.

Ghost: To sail slowly when there is apparently no wind.

Going about or tacking: Changing from one tack to another by going through the wind.

GPS: The Global positioning system used for accurately finding one's position anywhere in the world.

Granny bars: a strong structure designed for attachment or holding while working at the mast.

Gunwale: Upper edge of the hull.

Halyard: A line used to raise the head of any sail to the top of the mast.

Hanked on: A method of attaching a sail to a stay by using metal hanks attached to the luff of the sail.

Harbor: A man-made or natural place where ships may shelter from the weather or are stored.

Hard point: A stout structural feature designed to attach a lifeline or handhold.

Harden up: Turn towards the wind; sail closer to the wind.

Hatchway: An entry doorway that can be closed with a stout cover in rough weather.

Head: 1. An antique nautical term for the toilet or toilet room. 2. The top edge of a sail.

Headsail: Any sail flown in front of the mast

Heeling: The lean caused by the wind's force on the sails of a sailing vessel.

Helm: the wheel or wheelhouse area used to control the direction of the ship.

Helmsman: A person that steers the ship or sailing vessel.

Jib: A triangular staysail at the front of a ship.

JVC radar head: The brand name of a popular marine radar unit. The head is the combined transmitting and receiving antenna.

Knockdown: The unintentional pushing a sailboat on its side by the wind.

Knot: A unit of speed: 1 nautical mile (1.8520 km; 1.1508 mi) per hour.

Landfall: The act of sighting or nearing land from the sea.

Landlubber: A person unfamiliar with being on the sea.

Lanyard: A rope that ties something off.

Lay day: An unexpected delay time during a voyage often spent at anchor or in a harbor. It is usually caused by bad weather, equipment failure or needed maintenance.

Lifelines: A sturdy steel cable supported by stout stanchions along the sides of the boat that is designed to prevent personnel from going overboard.

Liferaft: An inflatable, covered raft, used in the event of a vessel being abandoned.

Line: The correct nautical term for the majority of the cordage or "ropes" used on a vessel.

Loose cannon: An irresponsible and reckless individual whose behavior (either intended or unintended) endangers the group.

Luff: The forward edge of a sail.

Mainsheet: Sail control line that allows the most obvious effect on mainsail trim.

Man overboard throwing ring: A rigid or inflatable lifesaving device with a line attached for throwing to an overboard person.

Marina: A docking facility for small ships and yachts.

Mast: A vertical pole on a ship which supports sails or rigging.

Masthead: The uppermost point of a mast.

Moor: 1. To attach a boat to a mooring buoy or post. 2. To a dock a ship.

Mule: An alternate name for the lightweight drifter sail that is said to "pull like a mule."

Nautical Mile: a unit of length corresponding approximately to one minute of arc of latitude. By international agreement, it is exactly 1,852 meters (approximately 6,076 feet).

Navigation Rules: Rules of the Road that provide guidance on how to avoid a collision and also used to assign blame when a collision does occur.

On the hard: A boat that has been hauled and is now sitting on dry land.

Pitons: Underground volcanic lava plugs that are uncovered to become a towering shaft of lava.

Pollywogs: First-time crossers of the Equator and target of jokes and celebrations.

Port: The left side of the boat when facing the bow, marked with a red light at night.

Port tack: When sailing with the wind coming from the port side of the vessel. Must give way to boats on *starboard tack.*

Porta-Bote dinghy: A unique folding boat that facilitates carrying in a small place; used as the ship's tender.

Potable water: Water that has been cleaned for human consumption.

Preventer: A sail control line from the boom leading to a fixed point on the boat's deck or rail (usually a cleat or pad eye) used to prevent or moderate the effects of an accidental jibe.

Radar reflector: A special fixture to enhance the ability to reflect radar energy. In general, these fixtures will materially improve the visibility by other vessels with radar.

Reaching: Sailing across the wind: from about 60° to about 160° off the wind. Reaching consists of "close reaching" (about 60° to 80°), "beam reaching" (about 90°) and "broad reaching" (about 120° to 160°).

Reais: The plural form of Real, the Brazilian currency.

Real: Brazilian currency with a value of R2.40 per U.S. dollar in 2005.

Reef: 1. To temporarily reduce the area of a sail exposed to the wind, usually to guard against adverse effects of strong wind or to slow the vessel. 2. Rock or coral, possibly only revealed at low tide, shallow enough that the vessel will at least touch if not go aground.

Rescue line pack: A coiled line ready for use in retrieving an overboard sailor.

Rigging: The system of masts and lines on ships and other sailing vessels.

Roadstead: An unprotected ocean anchorage.

Roll: A vessel's motion rotating from side to side, about the fore-aft/longitudinal axis.

Roller furling gear: A device used for rolling a sail for stowage, usually mounted on the headstay of the boat.

Rudder: A steering device which can be placed aft, externally relative to the keel or compounded into the keel either independently or as part.

Running before the wind: Sailing more than about 160° away from the wind. If directly away from the wind, it's a *dead run*.

SSB: A high-frequency single sideband radio used for long distance marine communications.

SailMail: A computer program for sending an email over the high-frequency SSB radio.

Sallyport: A secure controlled entryway as the entrance to a fort.

SCUBA: A system for swimming underwater. An acronym for Self Contained Underwater Breathing Apparatus.

Sheet: A line used to control the setting of a sail in relation to the direction of the wind.

Shellbacks: Multiple crossers of the Equator and instigators of jokes and celebrations directed at the Pollywogs, the first time crossers.

Ship: Generally now used to describe most medium or large vessels outfitted with smaller boats.

Ship's Bell: Striking the ship's bell is the traditional method of marking time and regulating the crew's watches.

Shirley: The name of the ship's dinghy.

Shoal: Shallow water that is a hazard to navigation.

Shrouds: Standing rigging running from a mast to the sides of ships.

Skipper: The Captain of a ship.

Sloop : A single-masted sailboat.

Sole: The floor of a cabin or salon aboard a boat.

Stanchion: Vertical post near a deck's edge that supports life-lines.

Starboard: The right side of the boat when facing toward the bow, marked by a green light.

Starboard tack: When sailing with the wind coming from the starboard side of the vessel. Has right of way over boats on *port tack.*

Stays: A strong steel cable used to support the mast.

Staysail: A sail whose luff is attached to a forestay.

Stern: The rear of a ship.

Sundowner: Drinks served at the end of the day, usually with a bit of conversation.

Tack: Changing course to take better advantage of the prevailing wind.

Tell-tale: A light piece of string, yarn, rope or plastic (often magnetic audio tape) attached to a sail to indicate the state of the air flow over the surface of the sail.

Topsides: The exterior part of the hull between the waterline and the deck.

Track: The course of the vessel.

Transom: a more or less flat surface across the stern of a vessel. Dinghies tend to have almost vertical transoms, whereas yachts' transoms may be raked forward or aft.

Trysail: A versatile heavy weather sail that we fly on a second track on the mast next to the mainsail. We fly this sail at night as it can be flown in most all weather conditions.

Underway: A vessel that is moving under control: that is, neither at anchor, made fast to the shore, aground nor adrift.

VHF: Very high-frequency radio, a short-range marine radio used for ship to ship and ship to shore communications of less than 25 miles.

Virginia: The name given the composting toilet.

Wake: Turbulence behind a vessel.

Watch: A period of time during which a crew member is on duty. Changes of the watch are marked by strokes on the ship's bell.

Waypoint: A location defined by navigational coordinates, especially as part of a planned route.

Weigh Anchor: To heave up an anchor preparatory to sailing.

Well found: Properly set up or provisioned.

Wheel: The usual steering device on larger vessels: a wheel with a horizontal axis, connected by cables to the rudder.

Windward: In the direction that the wind is coming from.

Windlass: A winch mechanism, usually with a horizontal axis used to raise the ship's anchor.

WinLink: A worldwide messaging system that links the internet to amateur radio channels.

Winches: A muscle-powered mechanical device used to retrieve or retract rope lines used to control sails.

Windy: The name given to the WindPilot brand self-steering wind vane. This device steers the boat for most of the trip.

Wing-n-wing: Two sails set on the opposite sides of a sailboat is usually called flying wing-n-wing.

Yawl: A fore and aft rigged sailing vessel with two masts, main and mizzen, the mizzen stepped abaft the rudder post.

James E. Keen

Meet Bill Doar

As a construction engineer, Bill spent his working life on long-term remote construction projects. While working on Diego Garcia, in the Indian Ocean, he met his second wife, Normandie. She was stationed there as a member of a U.S. Navy flight crew.

Bill and Normandie married and settled on a canal on Whichard's Beach peninsula on the Pamlico River near Chocowinity, North Carolina. They bought a thirty-six foot custom steel French sailing sloop and christened her Advent II. Over a period of several years, Bill and Normandie customized their boat for long distance travel with backups of critical systems and solar panels to become self-sufficient.

Bill and Normandie in the Indian Ocean

Bill and Normandie sailed extensively locally and made trips to the Caribbean, Bermuda, and the Bahamas. They became experts at handling the boat, anticipating the day they would sail out an inlet in N.C. to sail around the world. They did that in 2003.

Captain Bill Dore holds a one hundred ton U.S. Coast Guard Master's License.

Bill Dore aboard Advent II

271

Meet Jim Keen

Circumnavigations of Sir Francis Charles Chichester and Joshua Slocum have always fascinated me. Later, I followed the circumnavigation of sixteen-year-old Robin Lee Graham in his twenty-two-foot sailing sloop. His book, *Dove*, tells the story of finding maturity and a seafaring wife.

I restored and sailed a wooden twenty-one foot Lightning Class sailboat, owned small runabouts, leased crewed and bareboat sailing yachts, and restored and sailed a classic thirty-two foot Vanguard sailboat, Irish Mist.

I have extensive experience sailing rivers and sounds of eastern N.C. However, an ocean sailing crossing had eluded me.

Jim Keen

After college, I became a Certified Public Accountant, practiced with a large national firm, and then ran my own CPA firm. I worked in a commercial construction firm, then owned and

Jim meets Jonathan. a Gallipolis turtle.

operated a construction company in which I built several McDonalds and other fast food restaurants. In the 1980s, I closed my construction company, obtained a Masters in Community College Education degree, and taught accounting, auditing, taxes, and computer subjects at a local community college.

After fifteen years of teaching, I took an early retirement and settled into a waterfront retirement community near Chocowinity, NC.